Alban Butler

A short account of the life and virtues of the venerable and religious mother

1735

Alban Butler

A short account of the life and virtues of the venerable and religious mother

1735

ISBN/EAN: 9783337257491

Printed in Europe, USA, Canada, Australia, Japan

Cover: Foto ©Lupo / pixelio.de

More available books at **www.hansebooks.com**

A
SHORT ACCOUNT
OF THE
LIFE and VIRTUES

Of the Venerable and Religious Mother,

MARY of the HOLY CROSS,

Abbefs of the *Englifh* POOR CLARES at *Rouen*;

Who died there in the fweet Odour of Sanctity, *March* 21, Anno 1735.

By *A. B.*

O Quàm pulchra eft Cafta Generatio cum Claritate: immortalis eft enim Memoria Illius: quoniam et apud DEUM nota eft, et apud Homines. *Sap.* iv. 1.

LONDON:
Printed with Permiffion and Approbation of Superiours. Anno M.DCC.LXVII.

PREFACE.

THE holy Providence of Almighty God shines forth infinitely adorable and infinitely amiable in all His Ways, sweetly conducting all Things to their End with unerring Wisdom, and irresistable Strength and Power. A Christian who contemplates with the Eyes of Faith the lowest human Event, is dazzled and struck with Wonder and Amazement at the bright Marks of eternal and unfathomable Love, Goodness, Justice and Sanctity, which he discerns in every Circumstance of the Divine Appointments. He is not able to express the Raptures which his Heart feels in adoring and glorifying the Great

Great and Holy Author, in the Confideration of the leaft of his Works. At the fame Time we confefs that His Counfels are unfearchable to the higheft Cherubims, and infinitely above the Reach of the moft fublime created Underftanding; and that amidft the Darknefs with which we are encompaffed in our prefent mortal State, we fee only the fmalleft Part of the Links in the Chain of Divine Providence, the great Springs in every Action being now concealed from us, and the Iffues hid in the deep Abyfs of an Eternity, not yet revealed to us. Neverthelefs, the awful Scene is fo far opened to us in our prefent State, as ftrongly to awake all the Powers of our Soul to the wonderful Myfteries of this Providence in every Event, and to call forth our moft profound Adoration, Fear, Love, Thankfgiving and Praife.

Other human Events are fubordinate, and bear no Proportion to the Sanctification and Salvation of the Elect,

Elect, the admirable Fruit of the Incarnation and Death of the Son of God, and the great Masterpiece of Divine Providence. The Consideration of this most singular Mercy in every Circumstance, must transport our Souls with Love and Gratitude. For what Christian Soul, that has the least Sense of her unspeakable Happiness, in being called to know and serve her God, can, without shuddering, cast her Eyes around her on the tempestuous Sea of the World, worked up and raging with the Storms of the criminal Passions of Men, and covered on every Part with the Wrecks of Souls, miserably drowned in Sin, and sinking every Moment by Crouds into the deep Gulph of eternal Perdition! In what Transports of Love and Praise must we adore that Almighty Hand which by the most gracious Mercy first separated us from that unhappy Mass, translating us from the Region of Darkness into the admirable Light of his Grace, by which we were called to know, and serve our God? Our sense of this Mercy will be incomparably heightened if we look back on our whole Life past, and take a View of the numberless Sins, Snares and Dangers from which we have been most wonderfully rescued and preserved, especially from the most dreadful of all Misfortunes, that of being cut off by Death in a State of Sin, which, perhaps, we have often narrowly escaped. With what infinite Tenderness and Predilection, and by what a continued Chain of wonderful Mercies and powerful Graces does God deliver us daily from those Dangers, in which Millions continually perish, stretching out his merciful Arm to save us, ready to conduct us with a strong Hand thro' the Waters which threaten every Moment to overwhelm us, to the happy Port of eternal Glory. *Unless the Lord had been my Helper, my Soul had*

had almoſt dwelt in Hell. (1) When we look on thoſe unhappy Souls which groan for Eternity amidſt the ſcorching Flames of Hell; do we not tremble and ſay to ourſelves, Accomplices with them, as we are, in Guilt, how comes it that we have eſcaped that unutterable Calamity? Only the diſtinguiſhing Mercy of God can anſwer this Queſtion: by it alone have we been hitherto ſpared. Why are we not with ſo many whole Nations involved in the dark Shades of Infidelity, or in the Mazes of the moſt deplorable Ignorance of the ſaving Myſteries of the Divine Mercy, and the moſt eſſential Truths of eternal Life? Why are we not abandoned to the Slavery of vicious Habits, and to a ſpiritual Blindneſs and Hardneſs of Heart? God alone is our moſt gracious Deliverer. There is no Evil into which any have ever fallen, into which we ſhould not have been plunged by our own Malice,

(1) Pſ. xciii. (Hebr. xciv.) 7.

had not the Divine Succour been our special and only Protection, as St. *Austin* frequently repeats. *The Mercies of the Lord that we are not consumed: because his tender Mercies have not failed.* (2) The Blessed in Heaven having happily escaped all Dangers, and triumphed over their spiritual Enemies, never interrupt their Songs of Thanksgiving and Praise, confessing that God has crowned in them only his own Gifts and Mercies. *Our Soul hath been delivered as a Sparrow out of the Snare of the Fowlers. The Snare is broken and we are delivered. Our Help is in the Name of the Lord, who made Heaven and Earth.* (3) Thus the Wife Man says: *They sung to Thy holy Name, O Lord, and they praised with one Accord Thy victorious Hand.* (4) They are penetrated with the most feeling Sense of the Divine Mercy in their Favour, by clearly discerning that God had done *all Things*

(2) Jer. Lam. iii. 22.   (3) Ps. cxxiii. Hebr. cxxiv.)   (4) Wisd. x. 20.

Things for the Elect. (5) That the display of all His glorious Mysteries, and all the Dispensations of His Providence, in the Creation and Administration of the Universe, for their Sakes are ordained and directed to serve the great End of their Predestination. In the Revolutions of States and Empires, in Wars and Peace, in public and private Transactions, in the Rise and Fall of Families, in the Succession of Ages, God has often in View one chosen Soul, in whom he is pleased, in a special Manner to glorify His holy Name, and display His Mercy and Goodness to Eternity. Prosperity and Adversity, every Event, every Circumstance of her Life on Earth, is appointed by Heaven, in infinite Love and Mercy, with a View to her Sanctification. *To them that love God, all Things work together unto God, to such as, according to His purpose are called to be Saints.* (6)

(5) Rom. viii &c.   (6) Rom. viii. 28

The continual Instances of God's extraordinary Mercies and Graces in these Respects, through the whole Course of our Lives, call upon us to make him our constant, most grateful and humble Acknowledgment of our essential Dependance upon Him, and of his unspeakable Goodness, by which He is every Moment so many Ways our most merciful and most powerful Deliverer and Protector. But, alas! we perhaps pass our Lives in an ungrateful and criminal insensibility, and by a shameful Inattention, suffer the most extraordinary Instances of such unparallelled Goodness, to slip by unnoticed by us. In order to kindle in our Hearts the warmest Sentiments of Love and Gratitude, and to know God and ourselves; his boundless Mercy and Goodness, and our Baseness, Miseries, Ingratitude and Weakness; we ought frequently to lift up our Eyes to God, then to turn them on ourselves, and by considering our Souls as eternal

Mo-

Monuments of God's Goodness, and *Compounds of* his most astonishing *Mercies,* stir up ourselves to break forth into the warmest Acts of Thanksgiving, Love, and Praise; and to invite the Citizens of Heaven to all Eternity, and all other Creatures, to look on us, to consider the wonderful Works of God in us, and never cease to praise His Name for us with their most profound Homages. *I will praise Thee, O Lord, my God, with my whole Heart, and I will glorify Thy Name for ever: For Thy Mercy is great towards me; and Thou hast delivered my Soul out of the lower Hell.* (7) *O magnify the Lord with me, and let us extol His Name together. (8) Praise ye Him according to the Multitude of His Greatness. (9)* Remarkable Instances of this Providence, though sometimes not greater in themselves than those wrought in our own Favour, set the Divine Mercy in a stronger

(7) Pf. lxxxv. (Hebr. lxxxvi.) 12. 13. (8) Pf. xxxiii. (Heb. xxxiv.) 2. 3. (9) cl. 2. &c.

stronger Light, and more sensibly raise our Attention and Devotion. Of this we have an Example in a Letter of St. *Francis of Sales*, in which he expresses the Transports of Joy and Gratitude, in which he adored the Divine Goodness, in the Case of a poor Servant Maid, whom he found living a fervent Servant of God, in a Protestant Family, in the Midst of the City of *Geneva*. From her Cradle Almighty God had preserved her from numberless Snares and Dangers, which had been continual Incitements to greater Watchfulness over herself, greater Fervour in all religious Exercises, and greater Fidelity in every Duty to God and Man. He could not refrain from Tears of Joy to meet a hidden Saint, who served God with a Purity and Fervour of Heart, seldom to be equalled in the very Sanctuaries of Piety, in a Situation destitute of the chief external Helps of Virtue, and amidst the most dangerous Occasions
of

of spiritual Sloth, Ignorance, Vice, and a Forgetfulness of every Duty, and every saving Truth. Of this merciful Providence we have a most remarkable Example in the Life of the Venerable Mother, *Mary* of the Holy Cross, who having been wonderfully converted to God, was 33 Years Abbess of the *English* Poor Clares, at *Roüen*, and died in the Odour of Sanctity, in the Year 1735. And as her Call and Deliverance from the very Gulph of Perdition, was an astonishing Work of Divine Grace, so was her Fidelity in corresponding with the same Grace. No sooner was she brought to the Knowledge and Possession of the Heavenly Treasure, than she thought no Care, no Precautions too great to secure and improve the same. She immediately fled from the contagious Air of the World, and made a generous Sacrifice of all its alluring Vanities and false Pleasures, in order, as much as possible in this Mortal State, to cut off the

most

most fatal Occasions of Danger, and remove all Obstacles to her spiritual Progress. She shut herself up in an austere Monastery, that by devoting herself to the most heroic Exercise of every Christian Virtue her Holocaust might be complete. Such a Fervour condemns our Indolence and base Infidelities, by which we pervert the Divine Mercies themselves into our most grievous Condemnation. Though we may not be called to a Religious State, we are all called and obliged to be Saints; and though the particular Duties of our Callings may vary, our End is the same. Whether we live in the World or in a Cloister; howsoever our Circumstances and ordinary Exercises may differ, we are bound to practise the great Means of Virtue, which the Gospel and the Example of Christ and all his Followers, press upon all Christians without Exception; namely, Self-denial, Obedience, Humility, Meekness, Self-examination, Watch-

Watchfulness over our Hearts, and all our Senses, Fidelity in every Duty, the devout Use of the Sacraments, and all other Exercises of Religion. Every Christian is bound to die to himself and the World, to crucify his irregular Appetites, to subdue his Passions, and to put off the Old Man, and put on the New, which consists in the Spirit of Christ; that is, of his perfect and sincere Humility, Meekness, tender Love, and burning Zeal, by which he bears a Resemblance to Him. Whoever falls short of this Perfection, at least in his unfeigned Desires and Endeavours, cannot be said to square his Life according to the Gospel, or to bear the Image of Christ, the Badge of the Elect. Therefore the Example of a virtuous religious Person, is a true Model even to those who are engaged in the World.

The Example of this holy Servant of God will strongly contribute to fix our Irresolution, to rouze our Sloth,

Sloth, and difpel our imaginary Fears. In Her we fee that Fervour makes even the greateft Aufterities and Labours light and fweet. We want Courage to afpire fincerely at true Virtue, or to undertake the neceffary Means, becaufe Pufillanimity is difheartened at Shadows, and the leaft Sacrifice feems to the Slothful a Trial of Blood. But true Refolution difarms every Enemy; all Difficulties difappear before it. Conflicts and Obftacles do but raife its Ardour, as Fire is not obftructed, but exceedingly increafed by meeting a Field of dry Stubble, or a Heap of Chaff. If the Practice of Virtue has its Labours and Severities, a true Love of God, and the Unction of his Grace, convert thefe into Delights and Joy. The Example of the Saints at the fame Time removes the Prejudices and practical Errors which reign amongft Wordlings on the Obligation and Rules of true Virtue. The falfe Maxims of the World, in this degenerate

nerate Age, seem almost to obliterate those of the Gospel, even in the Hearts of Christians, and strengthen the Excuses of spiritual Sloth and Pusillanimity. To discover their Fallacy, and disguised mortal Poison, we must study the Divine Truth in its genuine Oracles, and turn our Eyes from the Croud, which we see walking in the broad Way of Perdition, to contemplate the Lives of the Saints. That of our Venerable Abbess will furnish us with an Antidote, and will shew us that we must walk with the Few in the narrow Path of the Gospel, if we sincerely desire to be of the happy Number of those that are saved.

The Compiler of this Abstract apprehends it will appear defective and imperfect, and rather disappoint than give Satisfaction to an inquisitive Reader, both through the Scantiness of his Memoirs and Informations, and from his Want of Abilities to do Justice to so bright a Character, and

so

so sublime a Virtue. Only a Saint can draw the true Portraiture of a Saint. Only a Saint *Bonaventure* could present to us in the dead Letter the living Image and true Spirit of a Saint *Francis*. One unacquainted with the heroic Sentiments of Virtue, and the interiour Life of the Saints, is utterly a Stranger to that Spirit, which animates every Action, and every Sacrifice of their Hearts; much less is he capable of giving to Words that Life, which only the perfect Spirit of those sublime Virtues of Devotion, Love, Zeal, Humility, and the rest, that characterizes the Saints, can dictate or suggest. Hence we have often left this faithful Imitatress of the Saints to speak herself, that by her own Words, her eminent Spirit may be better conveyed, and make a deeper Impression on the Reader. If the Writer has incurred any Censure by depreciating so great a Virtue by his lifeless Narrative, he has at least been agreeably flattered with the Pleasure of of entertaining himself on so sublime and so edifying a Model of Virtue, produced in an Age, in which all Hearts seem frozen to the Divine Love, and the very Idea of true Sanctity is almost obliterated amongst the greatest Part of Christians.

Doctor *Bonaventure Giffard*, afterwards Bishop of *Madaura*, and Vicar Apostolick at *London*, who going from *Paris* to *Roüen*, was for a considerable Time spiritual Director of this holy Servant of God, three Years after her religious Profession, always retained the highest Veneration for her eminent Sanctity, and to his Death had no greater Pleasure than to entertain others on the Edification and Comfort he had received from her Acquaintance. He committed to writing an Account of the wonderful Conversion, the Circumstances of which he had received partly from her own Mouth, and partly from others, who were Persons of unexceptionable Veracity. This Narrative

rative I have in his own Hand, figned *Bonav. Bishop of Madaura.* This Venerable Prelate earneftly and frequently entreated the *English* Nuns at *Rouen* to engage fome one who might have Leifure to write the Life of this great Servant of God. He repeated this Charge upon his Death-bed to his Coadjutor and Succeffor, the Right Reverend *Benjamin Petre*, titular Bifhop of *Prufa*, who by Letters imparted this dying Requeft of his moft zealous and illuftrious Predeceffor (whofe Name will ever remain in Benediction) to Mother *Clifton*, the Abbefs who was immediate Succeffor to the Venerable *Mary* of the Crofs. The following Abftract of her Life is compiled from the Relation of her Converfion, written by the above-faid Venerable Bifhop, from a great Number of Manufcript Exercifes of Devotion, and Rules of Piety, drawn up by this holy Abbefs, and ftill kept in her own Hand, in her Monaftery at *Rouen :* from the Manufcript Diary

of

of the same House, and from the authentic Relations given by several Nuns, who had for many Years been her spiritual Daughters, and from some Persons of Quality, who had long been intimately acquainted with her, had often enjoyed her Heavenly Conversation, and been edified by the heroick Spirit, and Example of her angelical Virtue.

A SHORT ACCOUNT
OF THE
LIFE and VIRTUES

Of the Venerable and Religious Mother,

MARY of the HOLY CROSS,

Abbeſs of the *Engliſh* POOR CLARES at *Rouen*.

THE Venerable Abbeſs, *Mary* of the Holy Croſs, was ſo careful to conceal the Advantages of her Birth and Parentage, that none of her Religious Siſters were able to diſcover her Family during all the Time ſhe lived in the Monaſtery. It was clear, from many evident Circumſtances, that ſhe was of high Quality. It was no leſs certain that ſhe was born in lawful Wedlock, of which an authentick Evidence was ſent to the Confeſſor of the Monaſtery, in a Letter

Letter from *England*. And had it been otherwise, she would not have failed to alledge the Irregularity of her Birth, when she was chosen Abbess, to which Dignity it would have been a Bar without a Dispensation, which she never had, and never stood in need of. She often spoke of several Persons of the most noble Family of the *Howards*, especially of the two Branches of the Earls of *Berkshire* and *Carlisle*, with some of whom she lived in her Childhood, and from whom she received her first Education, though she never called them her Relations; and not only the *Carlisle* Branch, but also *Thomas* Duke of *Norfolk*, *William* Earl of *Stafford*, and other Noblemen of the *Norfolk* or *Howard* Family, have on several Occasions, spoke of her as being of it. The present Abbess at *Roüen*, the Reverend Mother *Margaret Teresa Vavasour*, and others, remember they have heard her say, that her Father was out in an Expedition on Sea, at the Time when she was born. And when she was grown infirm in her old Age, she said pleasantly one Day: *Children, you must not wonder that I am weather-wise, for when my Mother was with child of me, she was always*

at

at her *Window*, watching *Winds and Weather*. This Circumstance seems to have given Occasion to the Opinion which prevailed amongst the Nuns, that she was Daughter to Prince *Maurice* (a) by Lady Mary

(a) *Frederick* V. Elector Palatine of the *Rhine*, and Duke of *Bavaria*, elected and crowned King of *Bohemia* by the *Calvinists*, but defeated by the Emperor his Antagonist, died at *Mentz* in 1623. By his Wife *Elizabeth*, Daughter of *James* I. King of *England*, he left several Children. The eldest surviving Son, *Charles Lewis*, born in 1617, was restored to the Electorate of the Lower Palatinate, in 1650, and died without Issue in 1680. Prince *Rupert*, born at *Prague*, in 1619; and Prince *Maurice*, born *January* 6th, 1620, were settled in *England*, in Quality of Princes of the Blood, by their Uncle King *Charles* I. The younger perished in the Expedition which he commanded at Sea, in 1654: Prince *Rupert*, after having distinguished himself by his martial Exploits, both at Sea and Land, and by his chymical Studies and Discoveries, died at *Windsor* Castle, the Place of his Residence, and was buried in the Royal Vault, in *Henry* VIIth's Chapel, in 1682. The Princess *Elizabeth* born in 1618, was Abbess of *Herworden*, a Protestant Nunnery, near *Ravensberg*, and an Admirer of Philosophy and the Muses. She died in 1680. The Princess *Louisa Hollandina* was born in 1622, at the *Hague*, the States of *Holland*, and Christian Duke of *Brunswick* being her Godfathers, the former settled upon her a yearly Pension for Life, and the latter sent her, some Hours after her Christening, a Present of 10,000 Crowns in a Gold Box.

Mary Howard, whom they suppose him to have privately married a little before he Box. Her Conversion to the Catholick Faith we shall mention below. *Edward* Count *Palatine*, who was born in 1625, went into *France*, where he became Catholick, and married *Anne Gonzaza*, Daughter of *Charles* Duke of *Nevers*, and Sister to the Queen of *Poland*. He died in 1684. *Henrietta Maria*, born in 1626, was married to *Sigismund Ragotzi*, Prince of *Transilvania* in 1651, and died in the same Year. *Sophia* born in 1630, was married in 1658 to *Ernest Augustus*, Duke of *Hanover* and *Brunswick-Lunenberg*, made Elector of *Brunswick* in 1692. She was left a Widow by his Death, in 1698; was declared by the Act of Settlement in 1701-2, next Protestant Successor to the Crown of *England* after Queen *Anne*, before whom she died only fifty-three Days on the 8th of *June*, 1714. Her Son King *George* succeeded Queen *Anne* in *England*, had before that Time succeeded his Father in the Dukedom of *Calenburg*, (of which *Hanover* is the capital City) he inherited the Dukedom of *Zell*, in 1705, upon the Demise of his Uncle, who was also his Father-in-law, *George-William*, elder Brother to his Father: Of his four Brothers two were killed fighting against the *Turks*: the third *Maximilian-William* became a Catholick, and died a General in the Imperial Service, in 1702. *Ernest Augustus*, the youngest Brother, died Bishop of *Osnabrug*, in 1715.

To resume the History of the Countess Palatine *Louisa Hollandina*, she was remarkable from her Infancy for her Wit, Understanding, Candour, and Goodness of Heart, and by the Help of the best Masters, was possessed of every Accomplishment of her

he went Commander upon that Expedition at Sea, in which he perished by Ship-

her Rank and Sex. In the 34th Year of her Age, by conversing often with the Catholick Princess of *Oxfordre, Elizabeth* of *Bergues*, she began to be convinced of the true Faith: by reading several Histories she was exceedingly scandalized at the Methods by which Protestantism was introduced in *England*; and discovered many capital Falsifications in the Writings of some eminent *Calvinist Theologians*. She then contrived to have frequent Interviews with certain *Irish* Priests, by whom she was thoroughly instructed in all the controverted Articles, and she was entirely convinced by perusing a Treatise written against the Ministers of *Bois-le-duc*. She saw it would be impossible for her to embrace the Catholic Faith so long as she lived with her Mother, the Queen of *Bohemia*. She therefore took a Resolution, whatever it might cost her, to retire into some Catholick Country, and to become a Nun. This she put in Execution in the Beginning of *Advent*, in the Year 1657, being then 35 Years old. Being arrived at *Antwerp* she spent two Months in the Convent of the *English Carmelite* Nuns, there made her Abjuration on the 25th of *January* 1658, and received Confirmation from the Hands of the Pope's Nuncio. Afterwards embarking for *France* she landed at *Havre*. At *Roüen* she was met by her Brother *Edward*, Prince Palatine, who conducted her to *Chaillot*, near *Paris*, where her Aunt *Henrietta*, Queen of *England*, lived in the Monastery of the Visitation. The Queen received her, and ever after treated her as if she had been her own Daughter, and straight presented her to the Queen Regent,

Shipwreck, in a Hurricane not far from the *Carribee* Iflands, in *February* 1654. (which,

be-
gent, *Anne* of *Auftria*, and afterwards to the King. His Majefty fettled upon her an annual Penfion of 12,000 Crowns, and the Queen Regent made her a Prefent of a rich Set of Plate. The Princefs *Louifa* ftaid a Year in this Monaftery, to accuftom Herfelf to the Exercifes of a religious State, in all which, even in manual Labour, as making Hay, Needle-work, &c. fhe furpaffed the Nuns themfelves; in Fervour, Exactitude, Regularity, and Recollection. Through the Mediation of the Queen of *England*, fhe by the moft dutiful Letters, brought about a Reconciliation with her offended Mother, who at firft fet no Bounds to her Rage; but from this Time to her Death kept a frequent Correfpondence with her. The Year following the Princefs went to *Maubuiffon*, a Royal *Ciftercian* Nunnery, near *Pontcife*, feven Leagues from *Paris*. It was founded by Queen *Blanche* of *Caftile* and her Son S. *Lewis*, and Dame *Magdalen* of *Pezé*, one of the brighteft Geniufes, and moft virtuous Ladies of the Age, had fettled there an auftere Reformation of the Rule. The Princefs took the Habit 25th of *March* 1659, and made her religious Profeffion 19th of *September* 1660. She was from her very Novitiate a zealous Enemy to the leaft Mitigation in Difcipline, and chearfully embraced the moft humbling and moft painful Exercifes. For a long Time fhe fwept out the Church every Day; fhe went through the Offices of Sacriftan, Portrefs, and Sub-priorefs. Four Years after her Profeffion, by the unanimous Vote of the Community, fhe was chofen and named by the King, Abbefs; of which Dignity fhe took Poffeffion on the 14th of

No-

beginning the new Year only on the 25th of *November* 1664, upon the Death of the Abbefs, *Catherine Angelica* of *Orleans*, of *Longueville*.

She continued always to eat in the common Refectory, like the other Nuns, would ufe only an earthen Cup, and fo in other Things like the reft; would not lie in the Abbefs's Apartments, but in a little Cell without a Chimney, in the remoteft Dormitory. Though it was at a great Diftance from the Church, and to go to it fhe had to pafs thro' open Granaries, and often in Winter, thro' Heaps of Snow, fhe never failed to affift at every Hour of the Divine Office by Day, and at Midnight, unlefs hindered by fome dangerous Sicknefs. All her Penfions and whatever could be fpared of the Revenues of the Monaftery, was confecrated to the Relief the Poor, or to diftreffed Monafteries. It was her Delight to have for her own Ufe the coarfeft and oldeft Habit, the meaneft old Book, which fhe would not have new bound, and fo in other Things. When a Glafs of her Spectacles was broke fhe would not have a new Pair, but ever after ufed the broken Glafs pieced together with Sealing-wax. In a Word, moft edifying in all Things was her Love of Poverty and Humiliations, the Aufterity of her Penance, her invincible Meeknefs, the Tendernefs of her Charity, and her moft fincere Humility. In her long laft Sicknefs fhe had the *Miferere* Pfalm writ in great Letters, hung before her within her Bed, which fhe often recited with many Tears; fhe had alfo an Image of our Divine Redeemer crowned with Thorns, fo placed that fhe could always turn her Eyes upon it. When fhe was fo lethargick in her Illnefs, that fhe was fcarce able to anfwer a Word on common Subjects, before fhe clofed her Eyes again

of *March*, some Historians call 1653) (1) But doubtless many other Officers of the Royal Army were abroad at Sea the Year after again to sleep, yet from her awful Attention to Holy Things, at her Prayers or when some pious Book was read to her, she never seemed subject to that lethargick Disposition. After receiving the last Sacraments, she calmly expired the 11th of *February* 1709, being 87 Years old, bating two Months. A celebrated Lawyer pleading before the Parliament of *Paris* against her Successor, *Dame de Chateau-Morand*, to shew the Contrast, draws the Portraiture of the late Abbess, the Princess Palatine, as follows: " Born amidst the " Splendour of a Throne, she had renounced with " Joy the glittering and alluring Pomp of worldly " Grandeur, to bury and annihilate herself in a " Cloister. The Daughter of so many Kings, " far from exacting the Homages of Respect due " to her Birth, she refused the common Marks of " Honour which are always allowed to the Dignity " of Abbess. There was no Distinction between " her and the last of her Nuns: the same Table, " the same Diet, the same Simplicity in Furni- " ture and Apparel, &c." This Account of that Branch of the Royal Family may suffice to shew how improbable it is that the Venerable Abbess at *Rouen* could belong to it, yet be unknown to it in the Heart of *France*. It may, also, give some Satisfaction to those who were in that Mistake.

(1) See *Francis Sandford*, Esq; *Lancaster* Herald, in his Geanological History of the King's of *England*; published in *Charles* the IId's Time, and continued to 1707 by *Samuel Stebbing*, Esq; *Somerset* Herald, in his 2d Edition.

after the Battle of *Worcester*, whilst *Cromwell* was studying to extend his Conquests, and to settle his Usurpation, and whilst the Royalists were still in Motion, both to fly from his Power, and to form new Projects against it. Nor does it appear credible that the Queen of *England*, who then resided at *Chaillot*, and the other near Relations of Prince *Maurice* in *France*, should not have been apprized of such a Daughter, if he had any. Neither is any Mention made of any such Marriage in the Pedigrees of any of the Branches of the *Howard* Family. And this Doubt seems entirely removed by the unexceptionable Evidence given me by the Honourable Mrs. *Mary Plowden*, Widow of *Francis Plowden*, Esq; Sister to *William Stafford Howard*, Earl of *Stafford*, who had with her Brother, a Nobleman of great Sagacity and Learning, made particular Inquiries about the Family of this Abbess, with whom they were both well acquainted. This Lady, who died only in the Year 1765, and was then Eighty-two Years old, assured me that Sister *Mary* of the Cross was Daughter to Sir *Robert Howard*. That Gentleman married for his first Wife *Honora*, Daughter and Heiress of *Henry Obrien*,

Obrien, Earl of *Thomond*, by whom he had one Son, *Thomas*. He had several Children, as is frequently mentioned, yet the Names of no other Issue by this or any other Wife, stand upon Record in his Pedigree, which is very imperfect, or in the Herald's Office. The Name of his second Wife was Mrs. *Uphill*. The Name of his third wife is not set forth in his Pedigree, nor any where to be found. It is therefore no Wonder that the Name of this Daughter should not be recorded in a Pedigree evidently so defective. That she was brought up by and in the *Berkshire* Family is evident from the Names of Lady *Anne* and Mr. *Philip*, and Mr. *William Howard*, of whom she used often to speak, as Persons to whom she had the greatest Obligations in her Childhood, though she took Care never to call them her Relations. For she was always most ingenious in concealing her Family in the Monastery; and such was the Respect which all the Nuns bore her, that no one durst put any Questions to her which she saw would give her Uneasiness. Even a little before her Death a Letter came to her which she read, and immediately threw into the Fire,

de-

desiring, as the Nuns that were with her imagined, to die in Obscurity as she had lived. She had before in the same Manner destroyed all the Letters, which she ever received from her own Family. It appeared evident that her extreme Care and Attention to live always unknown, was the Effect of her sincere Humility. The present Abbess, *Margaret Teresa Vavasour*, assures that this Venerable Abbess told her in the pious Instructions which she was giving her, that she chose the remote Monastery at *Rouen*, because in it she hoped to hide herself for ever from all human Creatures, as well as for the Opinion she had conceived of its Austerity and Regularity. But notwithstanding all her Artifices to live concealed and disguised, her very Carriage discovered her to be a Person of Quality and educated such: for her Dispositions were most noble, and her Behaviour that of a Princess, even after her religious Profession, and joined with the most perfect Spirit of an humble religious Poor Clare: and when she was a zealous Superior, and a most tender Mother to all under her Care, she always loved particularly the Poor, so as to love to see herself poor, and to appear such.

The Earl of *Carlisle*'s Family, the youngest, but richest among the collateral Branches of the *Howards* of *Norfolk*, always took most Notice of her after her Conversion to the Catholic Faith, being themselves Catholics for some Time after her religious Profession. This Earl, by the Presents which he sent her to *Paris* after she had changed her Religion, enabled her to go to the Monastery at *Roüen*, though he did not know her Design of going thither. Even the young Lord, who was a Protestant, a Descendant of that Earl, came to the Monastery at *Roüen*, and enquired after her when she was dead; which when he found, he said no more, and went away. Lady *Mary Howard* of the *Carlisle* Family, who was mentioned sometimes by Sister of the Cross among her Friends in her Childhood, must have been Wife to Sir *William Howard*, Father to *Charles* Earl of *Carlisle*. (b) It seems how-

---

(b) William Lord *Howard*, third Son of *Thomas*, the 2d Duke of *Norfolk*, married *Elizabeth*, Daughter to *Thomas* Lord *Dacres*, of *Gillisland*. His Son and Heir, *Philip Howard*, was Father to Sir *William Howard*, who took to wife *Mary*, eldest

however, that she could only have sometimes accidently seen her in *London*. For this Branch of the *Howards* was then of the Catholick Religion, whereas the Abbess, *Mary* of the Cross, used often to say, thanking God for his singular Mercies to her, that all her Friends in *England*, among whom she had her Education, were either Protestants, or of no Religion, and that in her Childhood all her Acquaintance lay only among such.

She was born on *Holy Innocents* Day, the 28th of *December* 1653.   Her Birth.

Her eldest Daughter to Lord *Eure*, the Lady here meant. For they had no Daughter called *Mary*. Sir *William*'s Son and Heir *Charles*, was created by King *Charles* the IId, in 1661, after the Restoration, Baron *Dacres* of *Gillisland*, Viscount *Howard* of *Morpeth*, and Earl of *Carlisle*, and died in 1692. His Son *Edward* succeeded him in his Honours and was of the Privy Council to *William* the IIId, Q. *Anne*, and *George* the Ist, by this last was appointed one of the Regents till he arrived from *Hanover*, and afterwards first Commissioner of the Treasury, Constable of the Tower, &c. and by *George* the IId Constable of *Windsor* Castle, &c. His Son *Henry* was born in 1694, was stiled Viscount *Morpeth*; became Earl of *Carlisle* in 1742; had two Sons, *Charles* Viscount *Morpeth*, (who died before his Father in 1743, and seems to have been the young Lord who called at *Roüen* in his Travels, after the Death of the Abbess, Mother *Mary* of the Cross) and *Robert*.

Her Friends being all Proteſtants ſhe was brought up in that Perſuaſion, chiefly in Company with Lady *Anne Howard*. By this Circumſtance ſhe ſeems in her tender Years to have lived chiefly with the Counteſs of *Berkſhire*(*c*) probably after the Death of her Mo-

(*c*) *Thomas* Earl of *Berkſhire* was ſecond Son to *Thomas Howard*, Earl of *Suffolk*, a younger Branch of the noble Family of the *Howards*, Dukes of *Norfolk*. This Earl by his Lady *Elizabeth* (one of the Daughters and Coheirs to *William Cecil*, Lord *Burleigh*, Son and Heir to *Thomas* Earl of *Exeter*) had nine Sons, *Charles*, *Thomas*, *Henry*, *William*, *Edward*, Sir *Robert*, *Philip*, *Algernon*, and *James*. His eldeſt Son *Charles*, ſucceeded him in his Honours in 1669. Sir *Robert* reſcued Lord *Wilmot*, Lieutenant General of the King's Forces, when he was wounded and taken Priſoner at *Cropley-Bridge*, on the 29th of *June*, 1644; for which gallant Action he was knighted by King *Charles* the IId. He warmly engaged himſelf in the Royal Cauſe, as did all the reſt of his Family. After the Reſtoration he was in great Favour at Court, and a leading Member in the Parliament-Houſe. In 1678 he was made Auditor of the Exchequer; which is a Patent Place for Life; ſo honourable and lucrative, that uſually a Miniſter of State, when it falls vacant, looks upon it as the beſt Settlement he can procure for his neareſt Relation; it was even then worth ſeveral Thouſands a Year. Sir *Robert* was four Times married, and had ſeveral Children; but by the Failure of Iſſue in his Grandchildren, the large Eſtates of which he was poſſeſſed in *Suffolk*, and *Suſſex*, fell to the Heirs general, except a Part

Mother. When Miss *Mary* was taken out of the Hands of the Nurses, she was placed in a very genteel Boarding-school, where she learned all the Accomplishments of a Lady of Quality; here she had for Companions Lady *Anne Howard*, and another young Lady whom she often named, but whose Name none of the Nuns now living, can recollect. She sometimes related, that when they were all three allowed to chuse Masters, according to their Inclinations, she made Choice

her Education.

a Part which reverted to the Earl of *Berkshire*. His eldest Sister *Elizabeth* being married to *John Dryden*, esq; the great *English* Poet, Sir *Robert* lived in close Intimacy with the politest Wits of that Age, and wrote many Things himself. His Poems which are collected into one small Volume, gained him no Reputation, though they are superior to those of his Brothers, *Edward* and *James*. Mr. *Dryden*, his Brother-in-law, paid him a Compliment upon them in Verse, in which he commends the Sentiments; yet in other Places he refuses to allow his Versification to be a Production of a true Son of *Parnassus*. Sir *Robert*'s six Comedies make a separate Volume, and among these the *Committee* and the *Indian Queen*, are said to have a great Share of Merit and Genius: a Proof of which is the Rank they long held on the *English* Stage, where the Committee still continues to make its Appearance, though the Character against which its Satyre is pointed, subsists no more, nay, is almost for-

Choice of a *Latin* Master, thinking within herself, though at that Time a Protestant, that if she should ever be a Nun, it would be of Service to her. By this it appears that even then she looked upon a religious Life as a State wholly devoted to the most heroick Exercises of Religion and Piety, and that from her natural Love of Virtue, she entertained no unfavourable Opinion of it, though on Account of her Difference of Religion she could then have no serious Thoughts of ever embracing it. Her

forgotten, viz. the Enthusiasm of the Puritanical Zealots, and Enemies to Monarchy of those Times. Sir *Robert* was a Man of Pleasure, as appears by his Fondness for the Stage; and always a Courtier. The Political Principles which he had warmly espoused in the Reigns of *Charles* the IId, and *James* the IId, and which he had published in his *Committee*, he publickly abjured, and being made of the Privy-council to *William* the IIId, in 1688 was one of the most rigid Persecutors of the Non-jurors. In 1692, when he could not be much younger than 70 Years of Age, he married Mrs. *Dives*, one of the Maids of Honour to Queen *Mary*. See his Poems and Plays, also the Miscellaneous Notes, and Prefaces to the Works of Mr. *Dryden*, in four Volumes, 1760. V. 2. p. xxv. and in other Places; also *Langbaine*, *Jacob*, and *Cibber*, in their Lives of *English* Poets; and the *Companion of the Playhouse*, or Lives of our Dramatick Poets. T. 2. v. *Howard*.

Her extraordinary Endowments of Mind and Body, and her rapid Improvement in every fine Accomplishment of her Sex, made her even in the Bloom of Life, the Admiration of all who knew her, and promised her the highest and most assured Favours of the World, and every flattering Part of its Prosperity. Whilst her Relations and Friends eagerly pursued its false Blaze in the full Career of the highest Honours, Riches, and Reputation of Wit and Genius, she by a singular Call of the Divine Mercy, found true Happiness and Glory in a Contempt of these empty Bubbles. In her tender Age she renounced the World, her Friends and Country, to consecrate her Heart with the finest Genius, and the most shining Accomplishments of Mind and Body, a young Lady could appear possessed of, to the heroick Pursuit of Virtue alone. Shut up in an humble Cell, a Stranger to the World, and the tumultuous Scenes of its Vanity and Ambition, she looked upon Heaven as her only Portion. There she placed all her Comfort and Joy; there she dwelt in her Heart, far from Hinderance or Distractions, conversing with her God, and glorifying

rifying Him by pure Homages of Compunction, Love and Praise, and by the most heroick Exercises of all other Virtues. By these her Soul was daily more and more purified from the Contagion of earthly Dross, and exalted to a State of Purity in all her Affections and Powers, and of perfect Virtue, resembling that of the Angels, by which she continually made nearer approaches to God, the Fountain of infinite Sanctity. By anticipating the Functions of the Blessed she filled her Soul with Divine Lights and glowing pure Sentiments and Affections, and fitted and prepared it one Day to join their Heavenly Choirs, and enjoyed in this mortal State some Kind of Foretaste of the pure Delights which overflow in that Region of everlasting Joy: a happy Exchange for the base Pleasures and empty Amusements in which blinded Worldlings drown, defile and degrade their immortal Souls, on which God had stamped his divine Image, and which he created for much nobler and holy Purposes and Functions. The Sequel of her Life will discover to us some Part of that wonderful Chain of Graces and Mercy by which she was called and raised to so

in-

incomprehensible a Happiness, from an Abyss of spiritual Blindness, and will set before our Eyes for our Imitation, the Means by which the same divine Grace wrought in her the most faithful Correspondence to it.

As she grew up the Sweetness of her Temper, the Pregnancy of her Wit, the Quickness and Justness of her Understanding, the amazing Beauty and Comeliness of her Person, and the Genteelness of her Carriage, made her much admired and spoke of, without any Prejudice to that Modesty which added the greatest Grace to all her other Accomplishments and Virtues. Leaving the Boarding-school she returned to the same Lady, who seems to have been the Countess of *Berkshire*, who charged herself with the Care of finishing her Education, and introducing her into the World; and who treated her in every Thing as she did her own Children (*d*). Living in this Lady's Fa-

---

(*d*) *Charles Howard*, eldest Son to *Thomas* Earl of *Berkshire*, succeeded his Father in Title and Estates, in 1669. He married *Dorothy*, Daughter of *Thomas* Viscount *Savage*, afterwards Earl *Rivers*, and had by her three Sons and two Daughters. All these Children died young, except *Anne* the

Family, and almost constant Company, she was here again much taken Notice of on Account of her rising Genius, and the promising Appearance she made, in which there was something that attracted the Regard of all who saw her. To this we may perhaps attribute, in Part, the following Incidents, related by the Lord Bishop *Giffard*, in the Account he has left of her in Writing, and which he had from her own Mouth. On a certain Occasion, as she was going up to *London* in a Stage-coach, a Gentleman in the same Coach, who was entirely a Stranger to her, said: " Madam, remember I tell you,

elder of the Daughters. Upon the Death of Earl *Charles*, the Title devolving upon his second Brother *Thomas*, the Lady *Anne*, Earl *Charles*'s only surviving Child, became sole Heiress to his personal Estate, and was afterward married to Sir *Henry Bedingfield*, of *Oxborough*, in *Norfolk*, Baronet. In this most virtuous and zealous Catholick Family, she publickly embraced the Catholick Faith, was most devout and zealous in all the Duties of Religion, a great Encourager of Piety and a Mother to all in Distress. She died in the most edifying Sentiments of Piety, on the 19th of *September*, in the Year of our Lord 1682, of her Age 34. She was therefore born in 1648, consequently was four Years older than our Venerable Abbess. The just Praise of her Alms and other Virtues is read in her Epitaph in *Oxborough* Church.

" you, that God has extraordinary De-
" ſigns of Mercy upon you." Theſe
Words coming from a Perſon who appeared deeply penetrated with Sentiments
of Religion, made a ſtrong Impreſſion
upon her Mind, and gave her far more
Pleaſure than all the flattering Compli-
ments with which ſhe was often entertained. The ſame Right Reverend Prelate
tells us, that when ſhe was about fifteen
Years of Age, being one Day abroad in
the Lady's Coach with her Children and
their Governeſs, there came up to the
Side of the Coach an unknown Perſon,
whoſe Habit and Staff ſeemed like a Pilgrim's; this Stranger fixing his Eyes on
her ſaid : " The Bleſſing of God will light
" upon you, and upon none but you, and
" the Queen of Heaven protects you."
Having ſaid this, he preſently abſconded;
and was ſeen no more. The Governeſs re-
ſented what he ſaid, becauſe he ſeemed
to ſlight the other Children, who ſeemed
principally to have deſerved Notice, being in their own Coach, though they
were younger than Miſs *Mary*, by which
Circumſtance it is clear, that Lady *Anne
Howard* could not have been in this
Coach. It is remarked of the Lady
whoſe

whose Memoirs we are writing, that during the whole Course of her Life she had a wonderful fine Aspect, which drew the Eyes of those that beheld her, and that a surprizing amiable Sweetness and Grace appeared in her Countenance. Two of the Brothers of the Earl of *Berkshire*, the Honourable *Philip* and *William Howard* took the principal Care of her whilst she was at the Boarding-school, frequently visited her there, and made her many handsome Presents, both then and afterward, when she was with the Countess of *Berkshire*, and also when she was at *Paris*, as she often mentioned with a great Sense of Gratitude, though she always concealed that they were her Uncles.

Miss *Mary Howard* was 18 Years of Age, and continued to live with the same Lady, when King *Charles* II. who saw her at a Play, was exceedingly taken with her Beauty, and inquired who she was. This being told her the next Day, she was much disturbed and afrighted, and spoke to her Friends in Town about the Matter with the greatest Alarms. The Hon. Col *Philip Howard*, and the Hon. *Edward Howard*, her Uncles, tho' she never added this last Circumstance when she mentioned this Affair) and above

all

all the Lady *Mary Howard* perſuaded her out of Hand to ſteal privately over to *France.* In Conſequence of this Advice, ſhe ſaid to a certain Lady, her intimate Acquaintance, that abſolutely ſhe would go to *France.* " Well," ſaid that Lady, " if you will go, I will go too." Accordingly, ſo ſoon as Things could be made ready for their Journey, the Lady ſet out for *Paris,* taking with her this young Ward, who going a- broad, took the Name of *Tal- bot,* and a Daughter of her own, who was then ten Years old. *She goes to Paris and takes the Name of Talbot.* Upon her Arrival there ſhe placed them both in the great *Benedictin* Nunnery of *Val de Grace,* that they might learn the *French* Language. This Place appeared to Miſs *Talbot* a Kind of Terreſtrial Paradiſe. The Nuns indeed here live in great Auſterity and obſerve a perpetual Abſtinence from Fleſh, being a reformed Congregation of the Order of St. *Benedict,* upon the Model of that of the Monks of St. *Maur,* in *France,* and of that of St. *Vanne,* in *Lorraine.* The Piety and Devotion which the very Walls and Furniture of this ſtately Solitude ſeemed to breathe

in

in every Part, raised her Mind to Heaven. But the deep Sense of Religion, which the very Place itself inspired, was more strongly impressed by the Example and Conversation of its holy Inhabitants, who both by their holy Functions, and by the Spirit of Humility, Meekness, Simplicity, holy Love, Candour and Ardour in every Practice of Virtue, and every Office of tender Charity towards each other, conversed like Angels in a Human Frame. Particularly, in singing the Divine Offices at the Foot of the Altar, all the Powers of their Souls evaporating in Holocausts of pure Love, they seemed to vie with the Choirs of glowing Seraphims, which without Interruption, sound forth the Praises of God at the Foot of his Throne in Heaven. And in their whole Deportment it appeared that their Minds were under the strongest Conviction, and their Hearts penetrated with the most lively Sense of the Judgments of God, and of the incomprehensible Mysteries of his Love and Mercy. These sublime Truths, to which the young Lady had never hitherto given any serious Attention, she now began to consider in such a Manner as to see their Evidence, and their infinite

nite Excellence and Importance, quite in a new Light, and to be ravished with the Beauty, Dignity, and Happiness of our Divine Religion, and its perfect Virtue. These Things made every Day deeper Impressions on her Soul, enforced by the great Examples of Virtue which she had continually before her Eyes. For being naturally of a most sweet and teachable Disposition, and easily inclined to the Love of Piety, Divine Grace found less Obstacles in subduing her Heart to its powerful Influence and Guidance. The Devotions of the holy Season of *Lent* having affected her Soul in a particular Manner, on *Good-Friday* she would assist at the Stations of Prayer, which the Nuns made to honour the Stations of the Sufferings of our Divine Lord. On this Occasion she was so moved by devoutly meditating on those sacred Mysteries and Pledges of the unfathomed Love of our gracious God and Redeemer, that after having finished the Round of these Devotions with the Nuns, she privately fell on her Knees, and without Reserve dedicated herself with the greatest Fervour she was able to the Divine Service, earnestly begging God to strengthen and

her Conversion.

and direct her in the Execution of the holy Desires, with which, through his Grace, she found herself so strongly animated. Being now sufficiently convinced of the Catholick Faith, she made a firm Resolution not only to embrace it without Delay, whatever Sacrifices it might cost her, but also in order to make the Consecration of herself to God more secure and entire, to devote herself to him in the most perfect religious State. She made her Profession of the Catholick Faith privately in this Monastery, in the Hands of an *English Benedictin* Monk, and would have taken the religious Veil in the same House had she not found herself strongly called to a more austere Order, and a more private House, though the Abbey of *Val de Grace* has always been remarkable for strict Observance of regular Discipline. Our young Convert was from that Moment a Model of Edification to the whole Monastery; for she no sooner began truly to know God, but she burnt with an ardent Desire of living to him alone in all her Actions, in the most perfect Manner she was able, regretting bitterly all the Moments of her Life past, which she had lost in the Ignorance of her sovereign and only Good. When

When the two young Ladies had been some Time at *Val de Grace*, they were taken out of the Monastery by the Lady to live with her again in the Town *(e)*. Miss *Talbot* durst not acquaint the Lady that she had changed her Religion; which, however that Lady soon discovered. For perceiving that she would no more eat any Flesh-meat on *Fridays* and *Saturdays*, she

---

(e) This Lady is commonly called at *Paris* and in the Monastery Lady *Danby*, because she became afterwards most conspicuous under that Title, but at this Time she could only be Lady *Osborne*. *Bridget*, second Daughter of *Mountague Bertie*, Earl of *Lindsey*, was married to Sir *Thomas Osborne*, of *Yorkshire*, Bart. who was created Earl of *Danby* by *Charles* the IId, in 1674, and besides other great Honours, made Lord High Treasurer; with the principal Share of the Administration, in which his Name will ever be recorded in the *English* History. He was afterwards created Duke of *Leeds*, by *William* the IIId, in 1694, having been instrumental in his Match, and in the Revolution. He died in 1712, she in 1704. They had six Daughters, the eldest of which called *Elizabeth*, died at *Paris* unmarried. She lived there with Miss *Talbot*, and at *Val de Grace* desired with her to become a Catholick, and was instructed in the Faith. But when she left the Monastery was compelled by her Mother to conform to her former Profession, she being then only Eleven or Twelve Years of Age. The Year following Miss *Osborne* died at *Paris*, cut off by a sudden Fever.

she immediately suspected the Reason, and said to her, "I hope the Nuns have "not made you a Papist?" No Madam: she replied; "the Nuns have not done "it, but God Almighty by his Grace has "made me one, and I shall never change." It is not to be imagined into what a Rage this threw the Lady, and from that Moment she persecuted her, as it seemed, even to Death had it been in her Power. On *Fridays* and *Saturdays* she would allow nothing to be given her but Flesh-meat, that she might be compelled to eat it, which yet she constantly refused to do, contenting herself with taking a little dry Bread. On *Sundays* and Holydays the Lady locked her up in her Room, that she might not hear Mass, saying, that she knew she committed a Mortal Sin by missing it on those Days. As if any Thing can be a Sin which is not voluntary. This Lady, though she professed herself a Protestant, seemed by her Behaviour, and by what she often advanced in Discourse, to be a mere Sceptick in Point of Religion, so as to believe, or at least practise, none at all; which Circumstance made her Persecution the more unreasonable. She had sometimes been accustomed ed before to treat Miss *Talbot* with Harshness, out of Capriciousness or Jealousy, when she saw her more admired and caressed than her own Daughter. However, these were only passing Trials, which the Lady herself soon endeavoured to make amends for by more tender Caresses, and greater Tokens of Affection and Kindness. But Miss *Talbot*'s Change of Religion entirely alienated her from her, and so enraged her that it is not to be expressed what Severities, Threats and Reproaches the young Lady had continually to bear, and by how many Persecutions her Constancy was put to the Trial. Once this Lady shut her up with an Earl's Son, on purpose that she might be seduced and forfeit her Virtue, or at least lose her Honour. But Almighty God preserved her from that Snare, and they only conversed innocently together.

A certain *French* Clergyman of Distinction, who often visited the Lady, saw so much of the ill Treatment which Miss *Talbot* every Day received, that he had great Compassion, especially knowing she suffered all this purely for the Sake of her Religion. Finding no other Means of procuring her any Relief, he contrived an

Opportunity one Day, when the Lady was out, of making her Escape in his Coach, and helping her to take Shelter in the Abbey of *Val de Grace*. When the Lady had found this out, she threatened to make her Complaint to the King, so that the young Lady was sent back again to her, upon her promising to treat her in a more gentle Manner. Notwithstanding this, the Persecution of the young Lady seemed no way abated: and besides what she had continually to suffer by every Kind of harsh Treatment, the Lady ever after carried about with her two Pistols loaded with Balls, to prevent any other such an Attempt, saying she would shoot her if she offered to leave her House: even in the Night Time she made her lie with her, and had one of these Pistols in the Bed, which gave Miss *Talbot* no small Apprehension, for fear of some Accident. The Lady, however, was at length prevailed upon to promise she would allow her to go into some Monastery, and carried her to that of the *Benedictin* Nuns of the Holy Sacrament. The Bargain being made, and every Thing settled, just as Miss *Talbot* was ready to go into the Monastery, the Lady

ma-

maliciously asked the Prioress if her Walls were high enough? At this Question the other was so struck that she refused to receive her upon any Terms, imagining that she was a Person of light Behaviour, or that some Attempt might be made by others to carry her off, by which Scandal, Trouble and Distraction might be brought upon the Monastery. This Disappointment caused the young Lady many bitter Tears; but the Lady told her with Fury in her Eyes, that she had now done what she had promised, and that the Nuns would not take her on Account of her Misdemeanors and bad Behaviour. Thus, to her great Grief and farther Trials, she was obliged to return home with the Lady, who breathed nothing but the Spirit of the World and its Pleasures, and took Miss *Talbot* with her to Plays, Balls, and Operas. This would have been to many a more dangerous Temptation than the most violent Persecution; and it was doubtless a Stratagem by which the Devil endeavoured to weaken her Resolution, and by Degrees insensibly insinuate himself into her tender Soul. But Almighty God having taken entire Possession of her Heart, all these

Things were grievous Torments to her, and she sighed after nothing but the happy Opportunity of giving herself entirely to God, which Sacrifice she continually repeated in Desire, and every Day with fresh Fervour.

It pleased God at length to put an End to this long and severe Persecution. And the Lady despairing to overcome her Resolution, gave her leave, at her earnest Request, to go to the Monastery of *Regular Canonesses* of St. *Austin*, at *Chaillot*, near *Paris*. Some Time after this Lady having lost her own Daughter, who died of a Fever, as mentioned in the Note, went to see Miss *Talbot* there, and told her that she was going for *England*, and that if she would go with her, she would take her to *London*, continue her former Kindness to her, and take Care of her Fortune: but if not, that she would abandon her, and that none of her Friends would ever more take Notice of her, or have any Concern for her. The young Lady seeing herself upon the Point of being utterly forsaken, without any Friend to depend upon, or make the least Provision for her in this World, cast herself into the Hands of God, and told the Lady that

that she committed herself to Divine Providence, and would never return into the World. The Lady having received this resolute Answer, abruptly left her, and was never known to have inquired any more after her. Miss *Talbot*'s Relations in *England* were very angry with this Lady upon her Return, because she had left Miss *Talbot* behind her: And some of her Relations came afterwards to *Paris*, in order to find her out, and bring her back to *England*. And after many Inquiries, being informed that she was gone to *Roüen*, they followed her thither; but finding her in the Monastery and a Nun, and seeing that all Endeavours to restore her to her Family would be fruitless, they returned Home without making any Noise, which they apprehended would only turn to their Disgrace.

Miss *Talbot*, seeing herself thus abandoned by the Lady who had undertaken to be her Guardian, did not lose Courage, and God was pleased to send her a speedy Comfort, in Reward of her heroick Sacrifice, and repeated Victories over herself and her spiritual Enemies. For a young Gentlewoman of the same Age with her, who was Daughter to the first President of the Parliament, and very rich, and who had seen her at *Val de Grace*, made her a Visit at *Chaillot*. And such was the Affection which this Lady conceived for her, that she came and lived with her in that Monastery between two and three Years, providing handsomely for her in all her Necessities; she even offered to settle upon her half her Fortune if she would continue with her; but Miss *Talbot* finding her Desire of embracing a most austere, penitential, religious Order, grow every Day stronger, addressed herself to the Convent of the reformed *Poor Clares* of *Ave Maria*, at *Paris*, this being then esteemed the most austere Monastery of Nuns in the World; and such it may perhaps be still reputed if we except that of *Clarets*, subject to the Reformation and Jurisdiction of the Abbot of the reformed *Cistercians* of *La Trappe*. In the mean Time the *English Benedictin* Father who had received Miss *Talbot* into the Church, hearing of her Inclination, advised her rather to enter among her Country-women, telling her there was at *Roüen* a very regular Convent of *English Poor Clares*.

Clares. (e) This Information gave her great Pleasure; for she had never before heard of any *English* Monastery of such an Order; and so ardent was her Desire

to

(e) The Religious Order of *Poor Clares* was instituted by St. *Francis* of *Assisio*, in 1212, when he gave the Habit to St. *Clare*. His Friars he allowed the Liberty of eating Flesh-meat at certain Seasons, that they might be less burthensome to secular Persons, amongst whom they sometimes converse and receive their Subsistence. For the Sake of a like Conformity in many other religious Orders, in which the spiritual or corporal Service of others is a capital Duty, an abatement has been made of the Severity of perpetual Abstinence from Flesh, which (except in Cases where Charity requires a Dispensation) was an inviolable Rule of the Monastick State for several Ages, and is still observed in all the Eastern Churches. St. *Francis* not thinking such an Indulgence necessary for his Nuns, enjoined them a most inviolable Rule of perpetual Abstinence, which is observed by them to this Day, without the least Mitigation. St. *Francis* out of a Spirit of Penance, and of the most perfect Disengagement from the World, established his whole Order upon the Foundation of the most rigorous Poverty, even in common. Hence the *Poor Clares* (without a Dispensation in extraordinary Cases) never enjoy any Rents, either in Lands or in Funds, but live upon the Capital which the particular Fortunes of the Nuns bring in, or upon the Alms and charitable Contributions of the Faithful. Pope *Urban* IV, in 1263, granted the Liberty to some Monasteries of this Order, to receive

to accomplish her Resolution, and complete her intended Sacrifice, that two Days after she set out for *Roüen*, thinking every Delay, even of a Day, a great Loss. The

ceive and enjoy settled Revenues and Estates in common. These are called *Urbanists*. Some of the Nunneries of this Order in *England*, before the Dissolution of religious Houses, were of *Urbanists*, particularly their rich Nunnery in *London*, on the Spot which still retains from them the Name of the *Minories*, between the *Tower* and *Aldgate*. Other Houses of the *Poor Clares* in *England*, as they had no Revenues, are no where recorded, except some few of which we find Mention made accidentally, as the second Monastery of *Clares*, in *London*, of which St. *Agatha* was titular Saint, the Site of which is not now known. Some Authors imagine the *English* Monasteries of *Poor Clares* in the Low Countries and in *France*, derive a Succession from this House. For we are informed by F. *Angelus Meson*, in his *Certamen Seraphicum*, that F. *Stephen Fox*, Warden of the *Franciscan* Friars, at *Greenwich*, being expelled *England* in the 2d Year of Queen *Elizabeth*, 1559, retired to *Antwerp*, from whence with twenty *English Poor Clares* he went to *Roüen*, and soon after to *Lisbon*, where *Philip* II. then was, by whom they were graciously received: by his Command a Monastery and Church were founded for these Nuns, at *Lisbon*, in which F. *Fox* was buried in 1580, as P. *Parkinson* relates in his curious History of his *English* Province of the Friar Minors. We find no further Mention of these *English Poor Clares*, at *Lisbon*, and we meet with *English Poor Clares* soon after this

The Honourable *Philip* and *William Howard* made her confiderable Prefents at *Paris*, and the Earl of *Carlifle* (who was a Catholick) hearing of her Converfion, fent this at *St. Omer*, feeking a Settlement, and departing thence to build a Monaftery at *Gravelines*, which was completed in 1603. F. *Parkinfon* imagines that thefe *Englifh Poor Clares* returned from *Lifbon* to *St. Omer*, and that fome of thefe foon after went to *Gravelines*. But this Account, however plaufible, cannot be admitted: for it is contradicted by the authentick Records concerning the firft Foundation of the *Englifh Poor Clares*, at *Gravelines*. This indeed preceded the Re-eftablifhment of the *Englifh* Province of the *Francifcans*, which was brought about by the Zeal of that truly great Man, F. *John Gennings*. This Gentleman was a virtuous Prieft of the *Englifh* College, at *Douay*, Brother to Mr. *Edmund Gennings*, the holy Prieft of that College, who was crowned with Martyrdom in 1591, at *London*, and whofe edifying Life he wrote, printed in Quarto, 1614. Mr. *John Gennings*, and fome Scholars of the fame College, took the *Francifcan* Habit in 1614. By their Means the *Englifh* Convent and College of that Order, at *Douay*, was finifhed in 1617, and foon after they obtained a Bull of the Pope, by which the *Englifh* Province of Grey Friars, of the Order of St. *Francis*, was reftored. In 1625, in the general Chapter of the Order, it was allowed to retain its ancient Rank and Precedency, of the fourth in the Order, and fecond among thofe on this Side of the *Alps*, the firft being that of St. *Francis* of *Affifio*, the fecond that of *France*, the third

sent her a very rich Pair of Beads, which on this Occasion she sold for an Hundred Pounds Sterling. This Sum enabled her to undertake her Journey to *Roüen:* thither that of *Rome,* the fourth the *English.* In 1629 Mr. *John Gennings* was appointed the first Provincial.

 Though the *English Poor Clares* had procured an Establishment at *Gravelines* long before this in 1603, they could not be of the Number of those, who had taken Refuge at *Lisbon,* who seem to have died there without leaving any Successors; for we find no farther Mention of them. The Ladies who restored their Order at *Gravelines,* were young *English* Nuns, who had made their Profession in a Monastery of the Country, settled in the Archer's House, at *St. Omer,* as is proved from the Archives of both these Monasteries. In 1472, when *Charles* the Bold, Son of *Philip* the Good, was Duke of *Burgundy* and *Brabant,* and Count of *Flanders* and *Artois, &c.* a Colony of *Poor Clares* from *Antwerp,* was invited and settled at *Veere,* called also *Ter-Veer,* or *Camp-Veer,* a small Town in *Zealand,* This Nunnery was plundered by the Calvinists. under *William* of *Nassau,* Prince of *Orange,* on the 11th of *May,* 1572, when the Nuns after suffering many cruel Indignities and Dangers, narrowly escaped with their Lives to *Antwerp,* and thence by Sea to *Gravelines,* and soon after to *St. Omer,* a City remarkable for the Zeal and Piety of its Inhabitants. Doctor *James Pamele,* then Archdeacon, (who afterwards died Bishop elect of *St. Omer)* procured them a charitable Reception on the 4th of *August,* 1581. They were afterwards

ther therefore she went without Delay to the Monastery of *English Poor Clares*, commonly called at *Roüen Les Gravelines*, and petitioned to be admitted a Novice. *She goes to Roüen, and is admitted to her Noviceship.*

Re-settled in the Archer's House, and their Settlement was confirmed by *Philip* the IId, in 1592. In this House several *English* young Ladies made their Profession during the Reign of Queen *Elizabeth*, and growing numerous obtained leave to form a separate Monastery at *Gravelines*, which they effected in 1603. This is the Mother-House of the *English Poor Clares*, and seems the only one amongst their four Monasteries, which has on some Occasions accepted of the Liberty granted to the *Urbanists*, of receiving Rents. The Settlement at *Gravelines* was procured for these Nuns, chiefly by the Bishop of *St. Omer*, the Abbot of *St. Bertin*'s, and Mrs. *Mary Ward*, who made some Stay, and even entered herself Novice there, in 1605; but leaving that House without making her Profession, she commenced at *St. Omer* a Kind of establishment of devout *English* Ladies in 1608, which not being approved, she removed to *Munich*, and there completed this Institution, under the Name of *Jesuitesses*. She often crossed the Seas for these Establishments, and also instituted the House called the Nunnery of *York*. The first Abbess of the *Poor Clares*, at *Gravelines* was Sister *Mary Gough*, who had made her Profession at Nineteen Years of Age, at the Archer's House, and after her Removal to *Gravelines*, in 1609, governed the *English Poor Clares* there four Years, till her happy Death, on the 23d of *November*, in 1613.

This

Reverend Mother *Giffard*, the Abbess, made some Difficulty at first, because she knew not who she was, nor from whence she came. But the Confessarius of the House

This Nunnery grew soon so numerous that three Colonies were sent from it to found so many new Houses of this Order. The first was founded at *Aire* by twenty-four Nuns from *Gravelines*, who were desirous to live under the Direction of Friars Minors of their own Order. Their Establishment was procured by the famous F. *Francis*, of *St. Clare*, or *Davenport*, President of St. *Bonaventure*'s College at *Douay*, and Reader of Divinity there, and F. *John Barnwell*, Reader of Divinity in St. *Anthony*'s College of *Irish* Friars, at *Louvain*, both appointed Commissaries for this Purpose by F. *Joseph Bergaine*, Commissary General of the *Belgick* and annexed Provinces. On *Whitsunday*, the 19th of *May*, 1629, the Abbess, Sister *Margaret* of St. *Paul*, called in the World *Margaret Radcliffe*, who had made her Profession at *Gravelines*, in 1612, having sent two Colonies of her Nuns before, took her Lodgings with them in the King's Hall, at *Aire*, which the Infanta had lent them for the interim. So soon as their own Monastery was ready for their Inclosure, the said F. *Francis*, by a special Commission from the Commissary General, visited the same, and gave the Nuns, when he had settled them there, the free Election of their Officers. Sister *Margaret* was re-chosen Abbess, and had in her Community eighteen other choir Nuns, two Novices, and three Lay-sisters. On the 10th of *December*, 1630, in the first Provincial Chapter of the *English Franciscan* Friars, after the Restoration

House desired she would first see her, and then refuse to admit her if she would; saying she was of so modest, virtuous, and graceful an Aspect, that no one could

tion of their Province, held in the Convent of St. *Elizabeth*, at *Brussels*, with the Consent of F. Gennings, the Provincial, F. *Custos*, and the Definitors, it was incorporated into this Province, which was confirmed by F. *Joseph Bergaine*, Commissary General over this Province, having special Authority for this Effect from F. *Bernardin de Sienis*, Minister General of the whole Order. This Nunnery of *Aire* is the only *English* House of *Poor Clares* which is subject to the Superiours of the Order, and adopted into the *English* Province, the rest being subject to the Bishops of the respective Diocceses. Indeed a Nunnery at *Bruges*, of the third Order of St. *Francis* is in like Manner of this Province, and subject to its Superiours and Government. This was at first a small House, founded at *Brussels*, on the 10th of *August*, in 1621, by Mrs. *Catherine Greenbury*, under the Direction of *English Franciscan* Friars. She was chosen first Superiour. Their Number growing too large for their House, they removed for the Sake of one more commodious to *Nieuport*, in 1637, and in 1661, purchased the old Palace of the Counts of *Flanders* at *Bruges*, called *Princenhoff*, with the Privileges annexed to the Site.

To return to the *Poor Clares*, their Numbers at *Gravelines* being again too great for the Community to find Subsistence in so inconvenient a Situation, Sister *Anne Brown*, Niece to Lord Viscount *Montague*, a professed Nun at *Gravelines*, was permitted

could behold her without being struck with Surprize, and without conceiving the highest Opinion of her. Nor was he singular in his Judgment, for the whole

mitted to attempt the Foundation of another House of this Order, at *Dunkirk*, in 1652. This she effected with three religious Sisters, whom she took with her, *Mary Clark, Anne Anderton*, and *Frances Rockwood*; Sister *Anne Brown* was chosen the first Abbess, in *September* 1659.

The Nunnery of the *Poor Clares*, at *Roüen*, is commonly known in that City by the Name of *Les Gravelines*, because it is a Colony from the same House, which was settled there in 1650. For in 1644, to ease the Mother-house, ready to sink under the Miseries of the Times, after the Matter had been earnestly recommended to God by long Prayer, Application was made to the Queen of *England*, then at *Paris*, and to her Treasurer, Sir *Richard Fester*, and at her Majesty's Request a *Lettre de cachet* was granted by the Queen Regent of *France*, for permitting sixteen of these Nuns to go to *Roüen* in *Normandy*. At the Head of this Colony went, Sister *Mary Francis*, called in the World *Taylor*, who had made her religious Profession at *Gravelines*, in 1614, at the Age of seventeen, and had there discharged with extraordinary Prudence and Virtue the Office of Mistress of Novices seven Years, and of Vicaress eighteen, and had already spent thirty-one Years in a religious State. Amongst the other fifteen were the Sisters *Mary Magdalen Clare*, (alias *Browne*) *Lucy Clare*, (alias *Perkins*) *Margaret Ignatius*, (alias *Bedingfield*) *Elizabeth Petre*, (alias *Salisbury*) *Wenefrid Clare*, (alias *Giffard*) two

Brad-

whole Community was charmed with her humble and religious Deportment, and with the Simplicity with which she gave an Account of herself; she was there-

Bradshaws, &c. and with them Mr. *Robert Rookwood*, Confessor of the House, who was a great Assistant in making this new Establishment, and in settling in it the most perfect Spirit of Devotion and Penance. The House was put under the strictest Form of the Reformation, drawn from that of St. *Colette*, through the Interest of the Queen of *England*, then at *Paris*, and authorized by Letters Patent, signed by *Lewis* the XIVth, in 1650. These Nuns, upon their Arrival at *Roüen*, were lodged in a secular House, and there in *Jan.* 1645, Mother Vicaress *Taylor* was unanimously chosen Abbess. They observed Inclosure in their secular House, till the new Monastery being finished, the Abbess led thither her Community on the 9th of *October*, 1652. The principal Benefactors were Sir *Richard Foster*, Mr. *John Petre*, the City of *Roüen*, especially the first President of the Parliament and his Lady; Lord *Arundel*, who sent his only Daughter Pensioner to the House, where she afterwards made her religious Profession, the three Lady *Westons*, the Earl of *Portland*'s three Daughters, Sir *Henry Browne*'s Daughter, and other young Ladies, whose Fortunes helped to build this Monastery; but much more their Humility, Disengagement from the World, Spirit of Penance, holy Zeal, and fervent Love of God, formed the spiritual Edifice. No one contributed more to this great Work than the first Abbess, who during the fourteen Years she governed the Monastery was to it a singular Example

therefore readily admitted by the Abbess and the Community, and a few Days after (which she spent in the most fervent Preparation of her Soul for this Sacrifice) she ple of all Virtue. She died happily the 8th of *December*, in the Year 1658, the 62d of her Age, having established the strictest Observance and Regularity, which is still maintained in this Monastery.

Sister *Margaret Bedingfield*, who had made her Profession at *Gravelines*, in the Year 1624, the 19th of her Age, and been sent by holy Obedience to help to found the Convent at *Roüen*, in 1644, and been the same Year chosen Vicaress, was made Abbess on the 23d of *December* 1658, and by her perfect Disengagement from Earthly Things, perfect Charity, and profound Humility much advanced the Spirit of religious Perfection, and died the 6th of *March*, 1670, being Sixty-five Years of Age.

Sister *Wenefride Giffard*, who had been professed at *Gravelines*, in the Year 1633, and twelve Years after was sent with the Vicaress and others to found the House at *Roüen*; was chosen Abbess on the 13th of *March*, 1670, when broken with Infirmities and old Age, she resigned her Office five Years before her holy Death, which happened on the 23d of *November*, 1706.

Sister *Mary* of the Holy Cross, alias *Talbot*, was professed at *Roüen* the 8th of *September*, in the Year 1675, of her Age Twenty-three, was chosen Abbess on the 23d of *December*, 1701, and died on the 21st of *March*, 1735, the Eighty-second of her Age, and Sixtieth of her religious Profession.

Sister

she received the Habit with one Mrs. *Parret*. Whilst she lived at *Paris* she had taken the Name of Miss *Talbot*; but to be more perfectly concealed, after her Conversion she took that of Miss *Parnel*, under which she was received at *Rouen*, and the Nuns there long imagined this to have been her Family Name, though they knew it to be customary among *English* Catholicks of Distinction, to disguise themselves in Monasteries and Colleges, by changing their Names, especially in Times of Trouble and Persecution.

It is the Custom for Persons when they enter a religious State, to change their Name, to imply that they are no more the Persons they were before, being now dead to the World and themselves, and that they are become a new Creature in Christ. On this Occasion Miss *Talbot* took

Sister *Frances Benedict*, alias *Clifton*, was professed at *Rouen* in 1681, chosen Abbess 28th of *March*, 1735, and died 23d of *August*, 1756, of her Age Ninety-one, of her religious Profession Seventy-five.

Sister *Margaret Teresa*, alias *Vavasour*, made her religious Profession on the 8th of *September*, 1727; was chosen Abbess on the 26th of *August*, 1756, and still governs this Monastery after the Example of her Predecessors.

took the Name of Sister *Mary* of the Holy Cross, that it might be a Memorial of her singular Devotion to the holy Virgin *Mary*, and to the Mystery of the Cross. For on all Occasions she had recourse with particular Confidence to the powerful Intercession of the Mother of God, and considered her as her special Model of Humility and all other Virtues. Her most tender Love for our blessed Redeemer, and singular Devotion to his Cross and Sufferings, moved her to add to her Name the glorious Epithet and Title of his Cross. By the same she expressed her Love of Sufferings, and her Desire of consummating her Martyrdom of Penance. Though yet a Novice in the Paths of a spiritual Life, she had by her Fervour made great Progress, and already learned to relish and understand the sublime Mystery and Doctrine of the Cross, upon which turns the whole Œconomy of our Salvation. For the Son of God, who on his Cross displayed in the most astonishing Manner, the boundless Riches of his Power, Love, Mercy and Justice, and wrought the great Work of our Salvation, has appointed, in his adorable Wisdom, that

by

by bearing some Share in his Cross, we should attain to the highest Treasures of Grace, which he purchased for us by his Death. By bearing the Trials he is pleased to send us, and by the interiour Exercises of Penance, we learn perfectly to die to ourselves, practise the most heroick Virtues, which only Sufferings call forth, resemble our blessed Redeemer, tread in his Steps, enter deeply into his Spirit, are united with him, and enrich our Souls with his most precious Graces, and most perfect Virtues. The incomparable Honour, Advantages, and Happiness of suffering with constant Patience, Resignation, and holy Love, are perfectly understood by all the Saints; and the greater Progress a Christian Soul makes in the School of divine Love, and of perfect Virtue, in the same Degree the higher she advances in the experimental Knowledge and Relish of the great Mystery of the Cross. In this sublime Theology the Apostles no sooner began to be initiated, than they rejoiced that they were accounted worthy to suffer Disgrace and Torments for the Name of Jesus (2). St. *Paul* saw this great Truth in a strong Light,

(2) *Acts*, v. 41.

Light, and was deeply penetrated with it, when he congratulated his dearest Converts for their Sufferings, as the highest Honour and Favour of Heaven (3). In the like Sentiments St. *Peter* calls those happy who suffer Reproach for Christ (4), declaring that in them the Power, Glory, and omnipotent Strength of God are displayed, and that his Spirit resteth upon them. This the great St. *Chrysostom* wonderfully felt when in his Comments on the Epistle of St. *Paul* to the *Ephesians*, meditating on the Title of Prisoner for Christ, in which the Apostle so justly gloried in those Words; *I Paul, the Prisoner of Jesus Christ* (5): he cried out in a Transport (6), "It is a more illustri-
"ous Title to be a Prisoner for Christ,
"than even to be an Apostle, a Doctor,
"or an Evangelist. This is truly a most
"exalted Dignity, far beyond all regal
"Diadems and Consulships. One who
"loves Christ would esteem it something
"greater to be in Chains for Christ, than
"even now to dwell with him in Bliss.
"No glittering Ornament, no Honour
"can

---

(3) *Phil.* i. 29, &c. (4) 1 *Pet.* iv. 14. (5) *Ephes.* iii. 1. (6) St. *Chrys.* hom. 8. in *Ephes.* See him also, hom. 16. ad Pop. *Antioch.* p. 160.

"can be so bright a Glory as a Chain
"borne for Christ. If the Choice was
"now offered me of all Heaven, or of
"this Chain, I would stretch out my
"Hand and take the Chain. If I might
"be allowed to stand with the Angels
"above near the Throne of God, or lie
"bound with *Paul*, I would prefer his
"Dungeon. Nothing can go beyond
"this Advantage and Happiness. I do
"not call *Paul* so happy for being *caught
"up into Paradise*, as for wearing this
"Chain. Would you have rather been
"the Angel loosing *Peter*, or *Peter* in
"Fetters? For my Part I would rather
"have been in the Place of *Peter*. This
"Grace of suffering Chains is something
"far greater than to stop the Sun, to
"move the World, or to command the
"Devils." Such were the heroick Sentiments of the Saints, whose Example confounds and loudly condemns those nominal delicate Christians who walk Enemies to the Cross of Christ, and Strangers to this sublime Mystery, the great Secret of the Christian Theology. Miss *Talbot*, though yet a Novice in Religion, had already so thoroughly meditated on the Love and Sufferings of her

cru-

crucified Redeemer, and the sublime Maxims of his Gospel, and had walked with such Fidelity, and heroick Constancy and Patience in the high Road of the Cross, under the Trials and Persecutions she had met with in her first Conversion to God, that she was deeply penetrated with the Spirit of the Cross, and a true Sense of the inestimable Treasures and Happiness that are hid in Sufferings undergone for Christ, the spiritual Advantages which accrue to a Soul from them, and the incomparable Sweetness, which through the divine Grace she often finds in them, as Honey hid in the Combs. This devout Esteem and Relish of the Cross she expressed both by bearing that Name, and in her whole Deportment. For from the same Source sprang in her a perfect Spirit of voluntary Mortification and Self-denial, and a vehement Desire of embracing a crucified and penitential Life.

Self-denial a necessary preliminary Condition in a Christian Life.

The Life of the Flesh, which is a Slavery of the Soul to sensual Appetites, and the Life of the Spirit, or of divine Grace, are two Opposites, and mutually destroy each other, as St. *Paul* assures us.

us (7). Wherefore, to beat down the Ascendant which the inordinate Gratification of Sense threatens to hold over us, all who desire to belong to Christ, are bound to crucify the Flesh with its Vices, and to carry their Cross after Christ. This preliminary Condition is required both to strengthen our Victory over our Passions, and to dispose our Souls to the Practice of heroick Virtue. For as our earthly Body cannot be raised to a Life of Glory, unless it be first destroyed by natural Death, so neither can any one rise so as to live by the Spirit, unless he be first dead to a sensual Life, by the Crucifixion of its inordinate Appetites, and a perfect Disengagement of the Heart from all irregular Attachments to the Vanities and dangerous Allurements of the World, and of Sense. And the more perfect this spiritual Death or Crucifixion is, so much the more perfectly, and with so much the greater Ease, will the Disciple of Christ be disposed to live and walk by the Spirit. These great and essential Truths, which most Christians, deluded by the Blinds of Self-love, and their Passions, study to soften and adulterate, our

young

(7) *Gal.* v. 17.

young Novice had so well learned and relished, that her Love of Penance, and her Fervour in its most severe Practices seemed insatiable. As she had embraced the most austere Institute, out of an earnest Desire of crucifying in her Soul all carnal Appetites, she found all the Austerities prescribed by the Rule, light and easy, and far from seeking to mitigate any Part, it was her Study and Delight to give to every Circumstance its full Severity. Nevertheless, to avoid all Danger of Illusion, Singularity, or indiscreet Rigour, it was her Care to measure all her Practices of Penance and Devotion by her Rule, by Obedience and holy Discretion. Such a continual Martyrdom of Penance, some perhaps, will think more apt to discourage and afright, than to edify those to whom it is not imitable. It is true, that in most States the Austerities practised in several religious Orders, could not be attempted; yet such Examples are a Spur to our Sloth and Cowardice: and a true Spirit of Penance and habitual Restraint laid on our Senses, are essential general Duties of all Christians, especially Self-denial or inward Mortification of the Will. Nor are Opportunities

ties wanting in every Station of Life, nay in every Occurrence, particularly in the civil Commerce of Society, which is only entertained by continual Offices of Charity, and the Exercise of Humility, Patience, Meekness, Condescension, Obedience and the like Virtues, the most heroick Sacrifices of Self-love and our own Will. Even that constant Watchfulness over our Hearts and Senses, in which every Christian is obliged to live; a Fervour and Exactitude in all Duties, and a careful Attention to do the Will of God in all our Actions, are a perpetual War against Sloth and Self-love, in which no Success can be hoped for without great Courage and Resolution in denying and dying to ourselves, and such an habitual Practice of the same, as gives an easy Victory over the Appetites of corrupt Nature, which if not kept in Subjection by constant Restraint, by their own Weight impede or weaken the Exertion of Virtue in every Action. This Violence and Restraint becomes easy by Degrees and gives true Liberty, and that happy inward Peace, which richly compensates the Pains it may cost by the Comforts and Victory which are its Fruit. In a religious Life

this

this is so much the more easily acquired, as the Exercises by which it is attained are more obvious, more easy, and generally more perfect; furnished by the bare Observance of the Rule, if complied with in that heroick Spirit which it prescribes. Of this Sister *Mary* of the Cross was an edifying and wonderful Instance. By her perfect habitual Practice of Humility and Self-denial, her Will was so readily bent to obey the Call of every Virtue and Duty, and so perfectly subject and united to God, that his holy Will seemed entirely to govern her, and regulate all her Desires, Affections and Actions. Her Thoughts and Imagination were curbed by holy Recollection and Compunction, and all her Faculties, Senses, and Passions were restrained by the watchful Guard she kept upon them, with so great Ease that it seemed natural, and to cost her no Constraint or Violence. By a perfect Victory over herself she possessed her Soul with such a happy Command over its Appetites, that no one ever perceived her Mind to be ruffled by any sudden Motion of Anger or Impatience. And in the Serenity of her Countenance, the Sweetness and Evenness of her

her Temper, and her ready Obedience and Submission to others, every one discerned and admired the Peace, Humility, Meekness and Charity towards all which reigned in her Soul. This perfect Spirit of Humility and Self-denial, and this Victory over herself was the Foundation of the eminent Spirit of Prayer, and other sublime spiritual Privileges to which the divine Grace raised her Soul. So very few attain this high Gift of Prayer, because so few study truly to die to the World and to themselves, and to disengage their Hearts from the inordinate Love of Creatures. For so long as the Soul remains Earthly or Sensual, wedded to Creatures, enslaved to the Senses and Passions, neither can God admit her to an holy Union with himself, nor can his Grace enlighten her Mind, or kindle its pure Flames in her sordid and prostituted Affections. Mortification, however, is no more than a Condition, which by removing Impediments, and subduing inordinate Appetites, renders the Soul amenable to Virtue, and pliable to the Operations of higher Graces, the Fruit of the Spirit of Prayer. This

Necessity and Advantages of a Life of Prayer.

it is that perfects the great Work of the Reformation of the Soul, it purifies and enlightens the Understanding, entirely cleanses and disentangles the Affections, and enriches the Soul with all spiritual Knowledge, and sublime divine Virtues. This is the rational or spiritual Homage, or Sacrifice by which a Soul makes herself the Victim, and dedicates all her Affections and Powers to God, it glorifies him in a Manner most becoming his Sanctity and Excellence; who being a Spirit, is to be adored in Spirit and Truth. Prayer is also the Source or Channel of all Divine Graces, the Key of all Heavenly Treasures; the Omnipotent Instrument of the Holy Ghost, in the wonderful Works of his Mercy and Goodness, in transforming an earthly and sinful Creature into a pure and holy Seraphim. It scours off the terrestrial Filth, heals the Corruption and Disorders, and strengthens the Weakness of the Heart, and being the Commerce of the Soul with God, raises her up, and unites her to, and in some Degree, transforms her into him. St. *Dionysius* the *Areopagite*, or rather the ancient Author of the Works which bear his Name, calls

Prayer

Prayer a golden Chain, by which we draw God down to our Souls, or rather raise them up to him. In this Union of our Powers with him, our Mind is replenished with the bright Rays of his Light, according to that Oracle (8): *Come ye to God, and you shall be enlightened.* And our Affections are cleansed and kindled into a Flame from the boundless Fire of Love which God is: His divine Image is imprinted deeply, and formed every Day more perfectly, on our Soul, in the Transcript of all Virtues, of which he is the great Original, Fountain, and Model. It is chiefly Prayer which forms all the Saints, and their Progress in the Spirit of Prayer is the Measure of their Advancement in Grace and divine Love, that is, in all Sanctity. From the Spirit of Prayer is derived all the Beauty and Glory of the *inward* House of the Soul (9). By its Exercises she is made the living *Temple* of God, in which he is glorified by every spiritual Homage continually offered up, and blazing on the Altar of her Heart: and she reciprocally is enriched and decked

(8) Ps. xxviii. 6. See *Dionysius Carthusianus L. de Fonte Lucis.* (9) Ps. xliv. 14.

ed forth by him with every Gift and Grace (10). If she is saluted by him his *Spouse*, by the Spirit and Exercises of Prayer she is adorned as it were for the Day of her Spiritual Nuptials (11), in rich Bracelets and Jewels; clothed round with Garments of gold Tissue, with golden Borders, and a precious Embroidery of every rich Colour in the curious variegated Works of all theological and moral Virtues. If the Soul is compared to a *Garden* (12), the Spirit of Prayer is the Stream of living Water, which being carried into every Part, continually entertains the Verdure of the Walks and Parterres, and the Beauty and Vigour of the Trees, Plants, and Flowers, which droop and fade if it fails, and are revived and flourish in Proportion as this Fountain furnishes more plentifully the Stream by which they are refreshed and nourished. In a Word, the Spirit of Prayer is the heavenly Dew, by which Virtues take root in the Heart, continually receive their Growth, and are carried to Perfection. Even the most heroick outward Actions of Virtue, derive their

Va-

(10) *Apoc.* xxi. 2.　　(11) Pf. xliv. 11. 14, 15.　　(12) Cant. iv. 12.

Value from the Purity and Fervour of Intention, which is no other than the Spirit of Prayer or its Fruits: Unless animated, and as it were seasoned by it, they cannot be perfectly sanctified. Those who take never so great Pains in the outward Exercises of Penance and other Virtues, foolishly sweat, toil, and waste their Strength, so long as they neglect to animate their Endeavours by a Life and Spirit of Prayer. The Reproach which *Jethro* made to *Moses*, is justly applicable to such: *You are spent with a foolish (i. e.* useless*) Labour, you and the People that is with you* (13). The most fervent Souls, in whatever State or Functions they may be engaged, even those of the most holy Apostolick Ministry, wander from the Path of true Virtue and Christian Perfection, if they suffer themselves to be withdrawn by the Advice of mistaken Guides, from the assiduous Practice of fervent interiour Prayer. Of this we have remarkable Instances in the Lives of St. *Teresa*, F. *Balthassar Alvarez*, &c. This is unanimously taught and laid down by St. *Bernard*, *John* of *Avila*, *Lewis* of *Granada*, and all other ancient and modern Saints, and the most experienced

(13) *Exod.* xviii. 18.   Mas-

Masters of the Rules of a spiritual Life, as a fundamental Maxim in the School of Christ, and of perfect Virtue. This is set forth at large by Doctor *James Perez*, the most eminent and pious Disciple of the Venerable *John* of *Avila*, in his Treatise *On Prayer*: who confirms the same by appealing to all the holy Rules of the Gospel; the Example of the Saints of all Ages, and the Experience of all who have any Acquaintance in the Direction of Souls in the Paths of eminent Virtue. The same great Servant of God assures us, that he was acquainted with a great Number of all Conditions, Princes, Dukes, Courtiers, Governors, Officers, Soldiers, Gentlemen, Tradesmen, Countrymen, Labourers, Handicraftsmen, Shepherds, Servants, and Slaves, who in the Midst of their Employs, which scarce left several of them a Quarter of an Hour a Day for close Retirement, were favoured with a sublime Spirit of Prayer, and lived in a constant Union of their Souls with God, by which they found great Comfort, Light, and Joy, under all Difficulties, and amidst their most distracting Occupations, Fatigues and Duties, in all which none were more Diligent and Assiduous.

fiduous. Amongst these several seemed to vie in Sanctity and Virtue with those holy Monks, who by their extraordinary Gift of Prayer served God in the Deserts with the Purity and Fervour of terrestrial Angels. It is a deplorable Proof of the Decay of Piety among Christians in this degenerate Age, that its most essential Maxims are made a Subject of Ridicule, in so much that a Life of Prayer and Devotion stands in need of an Apology. By many in the World it is ascribed to Weakness of Understanding, though true Wisdom and Prudence, which as St. *Thomas* shews, is the Fruit or happy Result of all Virtues, and a Ray of that Light, which is God himself, is chiefly attainable by our Converse and Union with him, who is its Source. No one can be so extravagantly unjust, and blinded by false worldly Maxims, as to deny assiduous Prayer to be the Soul and principal End of holy Solitude and Retirement, which constitutes the Essence of a religious State. A religious Man, as St. *Bonaventure* says, if unacquainted with the Spirit of Prayer, and not assiduous in the daily Exercise of Mental Prayer, carries about a dead

dead Soul in a living Body, and his whole Life is wretched and unprofitable. Sister *Mary* of the Holy Cross sensible that in this consisted the most essential Obligation, and the Happiness of her holy State, upon her first Engagement in it, made it her principal Study so to acquit herself of this Duty of Prayer in all its Branches, that by this divine Exercise she might consecrate her Heart and whole Life to God, by continually praising and glorifying his Name, and sanctifying and enriching her Soul more and more abundantly, by new Treasures of his Grace and Love.

 The divine Office she considered as the most sacred and most indispensible Part of this Duty, it being the publick Homage of Adoration and Praise which the whole Church joins in rendering to God by the Mouth of her Ministers and People. The Hours of Tierce, Sext, None, and Vespers, were appointed for publick Prayer in the Jewish Synagogue. For the Jews divided the Day by these Intervals of Time, of three Hours each, and the Night in like Manner by the four Watches, each of three Hours. It is most just that the Tribute

Church-Office.

bute of Praise be paid to God on Earth without Intermission, as much as the Condition of this Mortal State will allow. It was therefore offered at every Interval of Hours in the Temple. The Apostles observed these Hours of publick Prayer (14). The same were retained in the primitive Church, and are called by *Tertullian* (15), and in the Apostolick Constitutions (16); the Apostolical Hours of Prayer, Prime which is mentioned by *Cassian* (17), and Compline, mentioned by *Cassian* and St. *Benedict*, were added to begin and close the Day, by a publick Homage besides that of private Devotions, in Imitation of the Morning and Evening Sacrifice of the Old Law.

The primitive Christians, even the Laity, rose also in the Night to pray (18). Bishops, when in travelling they could not assist at the Night Hours in Church, still rose and kept them in their Lodgings (19). Mention is made of the Night

Of-

(14) *Acts*, iii. 1. &c. (15) *Tert*. de jejunio, c. 10. p. 549. (16) *Const*. Ap. l. 8. c. 30. (17) *Cass*. Instit. l. 3. c. 4. See also St. *Athan*. l. de Virginit. (18) *Lucian* vel alius in *Philop*. Plin. l. 10. *Ep*. 97. *Ammian*. *Marcell*. l. 28. St. *Justin*. *Tert*. Orig. S. *Cypr*. l. de Orat. Dom. *Euseb*. *Cæsar*: &c. (19) *Pallad*. in vita, St. *Chrys*.

Office in the Life of St. *Pachomius*, and other primitive Monks. For some Part of the Middle Ages the Devout Part of the Laity, especially amongst the Nobility, joined the Clergy in assisting at the Night Offices, as appears from many Instances mentioned in Church History, as of *Ebroin*, *Maire* of the Palace, &c. But in the Time of St. *Peter Damian*, only the Clergy rose to the Night Office, though the Laity who were not hindered, attended at the Hours of the Diurnal Office; and that holy Prelate exhorted a Nobleman, when he was not able to go to the Church, as in Travelling, not to fail to supply this by reciting at each canonical Hour a certain Number of Our Fathers (20) St. *Thomas Aquinas* says, that the three Nocturns of Matins were anciently recited at the three Watches of the Night (21). *Cassian* tells us, that this was the Practice of the Monks of *Egypt* on *Sundays* (22), when they met together. They probably observed the same Rule

in

(20) St. *Pet. Dam.* Opusc. Fleur. l. 61. Hist. See Card. *Bona* de div. Psalmod. l. 1. c. i. & iii. *Thomassin*, Merati, &c. (21) St. *Tho.* lect. 6. in 1 *Cor.* c. 14. See *Baron.* ad an. 51. n. 69. Suar de Relig. t. 2. l. 4. c. 4. *Bona* Psalmod l. 1. c. 4. (22) *Cassian*. l. 3. c. 3.

in private in their Cells, on other Days. It is evident from the Rule of St. *Columbanus* (23), that this was practised at least in some Monasteries in the West. Lauds when separated from Matins, were sung at Break of Day: Prime at Sun-rise. The Custom of the Nocturnal Office was grounded in the Exhortations of the Psalmist, to praise God in the Night. Secondly, in a fervent Desire of giving this Proof of our Zeal and Diligence, by interrupting our Rest, and conquering Sloth and Indolencce, to pay him this Homage; also that it might not be too long interrupted. Lastly, the Silence of the Night being most proper for Recollection and devout Prayer, pious Servants of God would not lose this Advantage.

The Divine Office is made up of the most perfect Homage of our Hearts, by most fervent Acts of Faith, Hope, Divine Love, Praise, Thanksgiving, Holy Zeal, Oblation, Compunction, and humble Supplication, with the most pure Sentiments and Desires of every other Virtue. This solemn Homage the Clergy is appointed to pay to God without Interruption

---

(23) *Reg.* S. *Columb.* c. 17.

ruption at the Foot of his Altar, in Imitation of, and in Union with those sublimely privileged heavenly Spirits, who stand always before the Throne of God (24), and whose Voice never ceases sounding forth his Praises (25). Religious Persons, who are professed to perform the divine Office in Choir, are in such Manner associated in this divine Function, as not to be distracted or interrupted by the frequent Avocations of the Duties of the publick Ministry, much less of Converse with the World or its Concerns. The nearer their Happiness by this Circumstance approaches that of the blessed Spirits, the greater is their Obligation of giving their whole Attention to this great Duty, which the *Cistercian* Monks, in their Rule, and in the Preface to their Breviary, call, with their great Patriarch St. *Bernard*, the principal Obligation and main End of the Monastick State. By it holy Canons and religious Persons, who are truly Men of Prayer, are the Angels of the Earth, and live united by their Function with the heavenly Spirits, nay, in some Sense establish an Heaven upon this Earth itself, in the Midst of that

(24) *Apoc.* i. 4. *Tob.* xii. 15.　　(25) *Isa.* vi.

that Deluge of Abominations, with which it is on all Sides covered. For in what does Heaven confist but in the Purity and Sanctity of its Inhabitants, and in their uninterrupted Contemplation, Love, and Praise of God. The Contemplation in Heaven is indeed intuitive and beatifick; that on Earth imperfect, through a Glass, in an abstracted State, and at a Distance. This, however, is justly called a Novitiate of the other, and those will be more abundantly filled from the infinite Source of Love and Joy for all Eternity in Heaven, whose Hearts have been more perfectly and more assiduously exercised in this Life, in the Exercises of divine Contemplation and Love, and more continually enlarged by holy Desires. Upon these Motives our young Novice looked upon the Office of the Church as the most essential among her Duties, and of all others, next to the adorable Sacrifice of the Altar, and the holy Sacraments, the most excellent and sublime. Oh! that those who, to the Dishonour of that God into whose Service they are enlisted, to the Scandal of the Church, and their own most just Condemnation, run to the Choir with-

without Awe or Attention, and perform carelessly this tremendous Office, associated as they are by it to the heavenly Spirits, who sing, prostrate, and veiled with their Wings before the Throne of God, were duly penetrated with the like Sentiments! With what Dread, Diligence, Zeal, and Devotion would they discharge this Duty, which they so shamefully huddle or yawn over, as if it were a Task! In this deep Sense of so sublime and divine a Function, Sister *Mary* of the Cross studied the Spirit of every Part of the Office, and the Rites and Ceremonies prescribed by the Church for duly performing it. To have ever come one Moment late, or not to have been sufficiently careful and earnest in her Attention to the divine Presence, and in every Part of the Preparation of her Soul for Prayer, she would have thought an unpardonable Crime of Sloth in so holy a Function. At Prayer she was penetrated with a most profound Awe of the divine Presence, as if she had been presented in Heaven before the bright Throne of the inaccessible Light of infinite Majesty. And the humble Reverence and flaming Devotion, which appeared

peared in her whole Attitude and Deportment; in her Eyes and other Senses shut to all earthly Objects; in her glowing Countenance, frequently bedewed with Tears, and in the very Accent of her Voice, bespoke an interiour Fervour of Soul, which might rather have seemed that of a heavenly Seraphim praising God in the intuitive Contemplation of the Divinity, Face to Face, than of one depressed under the Weakness of a Mortal Body in this State of Corruption and Sin: So lively was her Faith by which she contemplated the divine Mysteries, and saw him who is *invisible*, as if he were *visible* (26) and present to the Eyes of her Soul, and in whom she appeared wholly absorpt in Adoration, Love, Compunction, and an entire Annihilation of herself. She was particularly affected with every Part of the divine Office, every Canonical Hour of which, out of a tender Devotion to the Sufferings of our blessed Redeemer, she offered, amongst other pious Intentions, to honour the different Stations of his sacred Passion. The Law and Custom of rising to the Midnight Office pleased her

(26) Hebr. xi. 27.

her above the other Parts, both that she might not fall short of the Fervour of the primitive Church, and of so many Saints, and because the Silence of the Night helped her Recollection, and inflamed her Fervour, and the Circumstance of not admitting too long an Interruption of the divine Praises, extremely gratified her Zeal. She carried her Fidelity to the least Circumstance and Ceremony in the divine Office, and all her Devotions, not out of Scrupulosity, but from a Spirit of Religion, the lightest Tincture of which suffices to teach us that nothing is to be looked upon as small in the divine Service. With what Attention and Respect do we see Princes served by their Attendants! With what Awe does diabolical Superstition prompt the most savage Idolaters to behave in the vain Worship of their imaginary Deities, dumb Stocks and Stones? And shall the most sacred Rites of the divine Worship, shall the most solemn Service of the living God, our most merciful Lord and Redeemer, be treated in such a Manner as to be made the Scandal and Reproach of Religion itself?

The

The due Performance of the divine Office, indeed of all other Duties of Prayer, requires an eminent Spirit of Devotion, which can neither be obtained nor cultivated but by an habitual close Union of the Soul with God. *Other Branches of Prayer.* This Sister *Mary* made her chiefest Aim, and the Object of her most fervent Petitions to God, with so much the greater Ardour, as she considered the End and very Essence of her religious State to be no other than the most perfect Life of Prayer. Her private Devotions she regulated with the utmost Care and Discretion; so that they excellently answered and filled up all the different Duties of Piety. Amongst these the Sufferings of our divine Redeemer, and the other Mysteries of his sacred Humanity, were always her favourite Object, both in her Meditations and vocal Prayers. In her whole Progress in an interiour Life, she reaped the greatest Advantage from her Affection for, and constant Practice of holy Meditation, the sovereign Influence of which Exercise over her whole Life appeared visibly in all her Actions. For, according to the Maxim of St. *Teresa*, she looked upon that Prayer as fruitlefs and liable to dangerous Illufions, which remains barren, and paffes not beyond bare Defires, fuch being in a great Meafure merely imaginary, and proper only to put a Cheat upon the Soul, that is fo unhappy as to reft in them. Not content with kindling the warmeft Affections and Sentiments of Virtue in her Heart, fhe never failed to crown them with effectual particular Refolutions; which fhe was no lefs careful with equal Fervour to carry into Execution. Hence by this holy Exercife growing in all fpiritual Science and experimental Sentiments of Virtue, fhe ever returned from Prayer filled with heavenly Light, in a feeling Knowledge of the Myfteries of the divine Love and Mercy, of God's Immenfity, and her own Nothingnefs and Miferies; and glowing with Zeal for the divine Honour, and the Advancement of the Kingdom of his Love by the Crucifixion of Self-love in her own Heart: more humble, more meek, more patient and obedient: the Fruit of which immediately appeared in her Words and Actions.

In order to live every Moment to God alone, and make all her Actions an uninterrupted Chain of Virtue, and a continued

tinued Holocaust of herself and all her Faculties and Works to God, she had always in View the most perfect Accomplishment of his holy Will. To renew this Oblation of every Action with the entire Consecration of herself to him, she began every Prayer and other Work by earnestly begging of God in a fervent Aspiration, that he would inspire and strengthen her by that Prayer (or other Work) to glorify him by the perfect Sacrifice of her Heart, with all her Powers, and with her whole Strength, in that Manner which would be most to his divine Honour; and that he would form in her Heart those pure Desires and unspeakable Sighs, by which he might be most powerfully moved to grant his most abundant Graces and Mercies. Nothing is of more Advantage in a spiritual Life than an Habit of doing every Action with a View purely to the Will of God, and an Attention to his divine Presence, and of frequently forming such Aspirations, if it were but by repeating: *Thy Will be done on Earth as it is in Heaven*; *i. e.* as readily, as perfectly, with like Fervour and Constancy. Or that of St. *Macarius*: *Lord, have Mer-*

Mercy on me, as in thine infinite Wisdom and Goodness thou seest and willest best. Or: *May I be all thine now and for ever more, through thy beloved Son, Jesus Christ.* Or: *Teach me to love thee with my whole Heart, now and evermore.* But such a Practice derives the Value which it gives to every Sacrifice, from the Purity and Fervour of the Desire to serve God, in which the Soul entirely dedicates herself to him. This habitual Consecration, which the Soul makes of herself to God, is virtually renewed in every Action which it directs, this total holy Sacrifice being comprised, imbibed, and as it were repeated in every such virtuous Action, as St. *Thomas Aquinas* shews, speaking of a religious State. But all the Sacrifices of Creatures bearing no Proportion to the infinite Majesty of God, it is necessary always to call in the Merits of Christ, which being infinite, are an adequate Homage to the Deity. Though Man is Corruption and Baseness, his Offerings, made through Christ, and in Union with his adorable Sacrifice, will be accepted of by God. For *he hath made us acceptable in his beloved Son* (27). In this View Sister

---

(27) *Ephes.* i. 6.

ter *Mary* of the Cross, not superficially, or inattentively, but with the most lively Devotion and Confidence, closed every Prayer with those Words of the Church, *Through Christ our Lord*, or the like; and always made the Tender of her Heart and Actions to God, in Union with Christ's Sufferings and Death, or of his adorable Zeal or Intention of glorifying his Father, according to his immense Greatness, by an infinite Homage, in every Prayer and Action of his sacred Life on Earth.

Silence and Recollection being an essential Part of an interiour Life, or a Life hid in God, (that is, a Life of Prayer) and an indispensible Duty of a religious State, especially, in the holy Order of St. *Francis*, in which it is strongly enjoined and enforced by the Founders, St. *Francis* and St. *Clare*; this faithful Novice inherited the highest Esteem of that great Virtue, and Means of Christian Perfection. Superfluous or idle Conversation is a Source of numberless Failings and Sins, and a fatal Poison to an interiour Life, and the close Union of a Heart with God. It feeds and strengthens a

Love of Silence and Retirement.

Thou-

Thousand petty Passions, particularly, of Vanity, Pride, and Self-love, and is usually among Worldlings, a mutual imperceptible Communication of their secret Poison. It dissipates the Mind, and fills it with a Thousand vain Images, and the Heart with idle Desires, by which it is disposed to contract irregular Attachments, which raise a Wall of Separation between the Soul and God. Perpetual Solitude or Silence is in those, who have not embraced a State in which it is practised, incompatible with many social Duties; and it is what very few are capable of bearing, especially of the Female Sex: but even to see others now and then is a Relief to the Mind, and to interchange sometimes a Word or two may suffice. And one, who has begun to learn the divine Art of conversing interiourly with God, soon loathes all Conversation which does not raise the Heart thither. This was most remarkable and edifying in our pious Servant of God. Even on spiritual Subjects she chose rather to listen to others than to speak much herself, and what she said was delivered with the greatest Modesty, and in few Words. Even in Times of Recreation her Discourse seemed ed confined to the Offices of Charity and Necessity; her Words were always seasoned with an extraordinary Spirit of Piety and Humility, and bespoke her Soul absorpt in God, and penetrated with the awful Sense of his divine Presence. Particularly, she never let drop the least Word of Complaint or Anger, and never spoke to others of her Sufferings in any kind, unless when obliged by some Necessity, or to ask Advice. Upon meeting with any Difficulty or Cross, she immediately recollected herself, renewed her Spirit interiourly in God, stirred herself up sweetly to bear it with Courage and Cheerfulness; adored, and as it were, kissed the Hand of his divine Providence with perfect Submission to his merciful Appointments, and hastened to hide herself with her little Cross in the Heart of Jesus, that she might learn to bear it with him, and for his Love. In the Sanctuary of his divine Heart she found all Sweetness and Comfort: we in vain seek for it in Creatures, which, instead of affording any Ease, can only increase our Trouble and Pain. To study and put on the Spirit of Christ, she meditated daily on some of the adore-

F *able*

able Mysteries of his divine Life, entertained herself frequently on them in the Day by devout Aspirations, endeavouring never to act or think but with him, and in his Spirit. The Virtues themselves, and the whole Lives of most Christians, are full of Imperfection, Infidelities and Sin, because they give little heed to their Interiour, and are careless in watching over it, and regulating the inward Motions, Desires, and Affections of their Soul. By diligent Self-examination, Watchfulness over her Heart and Senses, and Compunction; and by holy Meditation, Prayer, and conversing with God, this his true Servant so governed and quickened her Interiour, that animated with the fervent and perfect Spirit of all Virtue she produced in all her Actions continual Fruits of Humility, Zeal, Charity, and other Virtues, and her whole Conversation seemed a perfect Model of a religious State, or the Rule of evangelical Perfection, exemplified in Practice.

Her religious Profession.

A Novice so accomplished in all Virtue was readily admitted by the unanimous Votes of the Community to make her religious Profession, and the Year of her No-

Noviciate being expired, after the regular Examination of her Vocation by the great Vicar by Virtue of a Commission of the Archbishop, she pronounced her solemn Vows on the Feast of the Nativity of the Blessed Virgin, in the Year 1675. From what has been already said it may be better imagined than described with what Fervour and Humility she consummated her Sacrifice on that Occasion. St. *Teresa* one Day complained to our Lord that we no longer see among Souls which dedicate themselves to his Service, those wonderful Effusions of Grace, by which he formed amongst the primitive Monks so many eminent Saints and divine Men; and she asked him how this comes to pass since his Power is not weakened, nor can the Fountain of his Grace be impaired? He answered her in a Vision, that the Reason of this Difference arises from Men, not from him who is unchangeably the same. His Arm is not shortened, nor is his Goodness less desirous to communicate his choicest Graces: but we so contract our Hearts, as to shut them against him, and by our criminal Reserves remain incapable of receiving the extraordinary Effects of his Bounty. The Fault is wholly in us that we are so poor, so destitute of heavenly Goods. For whilst our infinitely gracious God makes himself all ours, and is ready to refuse us nothing, we obstruct the Designs of his Love and Mercy, for Want of Courage and Resolution in removing the Obstacles, and in making the Sacrifice of our Hearts entire. For so long as Self-love still maintains its Hold by any inordinate Attachment or Passion, the Reign of divine Grace and Love cannot be triumphantly established in our Souls. Our Sloth is the more unpardonable, inasmuch as this Reserve is often in the most foolish Trifle, in a nothing, which after all our good Resolutions we could never find in our Hearts perfectly to renounce. In one this is a silly Caprice or Humour, in another a Frowardness of Temper, in a third a disguised slight Vanity, or a petty insignificant Sensuality, Sloth, or the like. What a Pity is it, that after making the greatest Sacrifices we should fall short for the Sake of such Bubbles! To those generous Souls which give all to God, who courageously resolve to spare nothing that they may be altogether his,

his, he communicates himself with such an Excess of Goodness and Profusion, as to raise eternal Astonishment in the Angels.

With what heroick Dispositions of Soul Sister *Mary* made the entire Sacrifice of herself, we may gather from the Fervour of her Preparation, from the extraordinary Devotion and Humility with which she performed that sacred Ceremony of the solemn Dedication of herself to God, and from the Influence it had upon her whole Life and Deportment; to the last Moment in which she crowned her Holocaust. With the greatest Joy and Gratitude to God she now saw her most ardent Desires accomplished, and herself, by this solemn Act, as by a new Tie and Obligation, belonging entire to God, for ever devoted and consecrated to his Service and sweet Love. She therefore studied with all her Powers and her whole Strength to glorify him, and to do what was most pleasing to him in every Action. In this View she regulated the Manner of performing every Duty of the Day in the most perfect Manner she was able, and she made every Action a new entire Sacrifice of herself to God. But every

Day before and after Mass she fervently renewed the solemn Consecration she had made of herself in her religious Profession, earnestly begging to be accepted through, and in Union with the spotless Victim of the Altar, and to be powerfully strengthened by the divine Grace faithfully to accomplish the same by her Martyrdom of Penance. In this Spirit and perfect Fidelity she lived a *burning and shining Light* (28) to the Community; shining by the Light of the most lively and active Faith, in which she appeared to contemplate God with the most ardent and pure Love, and to be totally devoted to him in every Action: *burning* with holy Zeal for his Honour, so as to kindle in the Breasts of others, by her Words and Deportment, a Spark of that holy Love of God, which burnt in her own.

For some Time after her Profession she was carried on sweetly in the Paths of Virtue and religious Discipline, upon the Wings of divine Love, and plentifully fed with the Milk of heavenly Consolations; she ardently followed her divine Spouse in the sweet Odour of his Oint-

(28) *John* v. 35.

Ointments, crying out with the loving Soul in the Canticles: *I sat down under his Shadow whom I desired, and his Fruit was sweet to my Palate. He hath brought me into the Wine-cellar: He hath set in Order Charity in me* (29). And with the Psalmist: *My Soul shall rejoice in the Lord, and shall be delighted in his Salvation. All my Bones shall say, Lord, who is like to thee* (30). The Servants of God assure us, that so great is the Sweetness of heavenly Comfort, which God frequently affords devout Souls in this Life that it far surpasses all terrestrial Delights, or whatever it could come into the Minds of carnal Men to imagine, and that a Person here truly finds the hundred-fold for all he can have forsaken for Christ, besides the Reversion of that never-fading Crown which is prepared for him in everlasting Glory. For though the Reward is reserved for the World to come, Christ promises an Earnest in Hand, as Labourers receive their Wages when the Work is done, but in the mean Time present Refreshment and Support. This his Servants abundantly experience, not only in the pure and holy Joy which his di-vine

(29) Cant. ii. 3. 4.   (30) Pf. xxxiv. 9. 10.

vine Love and inward Peace afford even under the sharpest Trials, but likewise by the Dew of heavenly Consolations, with which he often refreshes their Souls, as a Foretaste of his eternal Banquet, and an Earnest of his Love. *The sprouting Plant shall rejoice in its Droppings* (31). These sweeten their Crosses themselves, and season their Tears with holy inexpressible Joy. " I am astonished, says St. " *John Climacus* (32), when I consider " happy Compunction, and I wonder " how carnal Men can think it Affliction. " In it is found a sweet Pleasure and spi- " tual Joy, as Honey is contained in " the Combs. God invisibly visits and " comforts the Heart that is broken with " holy Sorrow. St. *Chrysostom* writes: " When you hear Mention made of Tears " in Devotion, conceive not any Thing " bitter or grievous. They are sweeter " than any carnal Delights which the " World can enjoy (33)." And St. *Austin* says: " The Tears of Prayer are sweeter " than the Joys of Theatres (34)." If such

(31) Ps. lxiv. 11.   (32) St. *Jo. Clim.* gr. 7. p. 427.   (33) St. *Chrys.* l. de Virginit. t. 1. p. 321. ed *Ben.*   (34) St. *Aug.* Enar. in Ps. 128. t. 4.

such is the Sweetness of the Tears of holy Compunction, and God so tenderly wipes them off, can we be surprised at the wonderful Things we are told by the Saints of the incomparable spiritual Comfort and holy Joy which the close Union of a Soul with God often infuses in the Jubilee of pure Love and Praise. " The " Consolation of the Holy Ghost," says an experienced Author, " far exceeds all " worldly Pleasures, if they could be cen- " tered in one Man, and be all enjoyed " together. In it the Heart melts away " through Excess of Joy, and is not able " to contain itself (35)." This State is truly a Paradise of heavenly Delights. " The Soul of a Servant of God," says St. *John* of the Cross (36), " always " swims in Joy, always keeps Holyday, " always lives in her Palace of Jubilee, " ever singing a new Song of Love, " with fresh Ardour, and a Joy con- " stantly new." It is true these Favours must not be presumptuously desired or considered as valuable in themselves; nor must

---

(35) *Ruisbroch* Spirit. *Nuptiar*. l. 2. c. 19. See St. *Fr.* of *Sales*, on the Love of God. l. 6. c. 15. The Lives of St. *Ephrem*, St. *Fr. Xaver*, St. *Ph. Neri*, &c. (36) Flame of divine Love. p. 528.

must a Soul dwell or fix her Attention on them, but on the Giver; acknowledging them the Work of his pure Mercy toward the most unworthy of all Creatures, sinking deeper into the Abyss of her own Baseness, and trembling lest she abuse so undeserved a Mercy. At the same Time she is ready to bear all Trials, and prepares herself in Spirit for them, knowing this Vicissitude to be the Condition of this Mortal Life, and she is even animated with a Desire of suffering Labour and Hardships for the Love of Christ (37). Such were the Dispositions, and such the Conduct of our holy Nun, under these heavenly Visitations, which by her Silence, Humility, and Fidelity, she improved to her daily Advancement in the Love of God, attracted by the Charms of his Goodness. Her Love seemed already all Enjoyment, and the Road to Heaven was all so strewed with fragrant Roses and pure Delights, that nothing could appear rugged in it; her Life and all her Exercises seemed not barely a Noviciate, but at the same Time a Commencement of that Bliss after which she as-

(37) Imit of Chr. l. 2. c. 9, and 10. l. 1. c. 20, &c.

aspired. But *Calvary* must be passed over before we can arrive at Mount *Olivet*. To reign with Christ, we must carry our Cross after him: the Crown, which he holds forth, is not to be purchased upon any other Conditions.

F. *Lewis* of *Granada*, that experienced Master of a spiritual Life, makes this Remark, that Almighty God is pleased frequently to favour fervent young Novices with the Caresses of his heavenly Comfort, to engage them by this Taste of the Sweetness of his Love, and this Earnest of his Tenderness and Goodness, to run after him more chearfully *in the Odour of his sweet Ointments* (38), and to give them Strength and Courage under subsequent Trials. But these sensible Caresses do not last always. It is necessary that Souls whom God prepares to be chosen Vessels of his Grace, should still more perfectly cleanse and purify their Affections in the Crucible: in order to which he usually visits them with severe interiour Trials. The outward Persecutions which our zealous young Convert had suffered from Men, jointly with her habitual Practice of Self-denial, Watchfulness

(38) Cant. i. 3.

fulness and Compunction, had exceedingly contributed by the divine Grace to wean and disengage her Affections from the World, to promote the great Work of the Crucifixion of her Heart to it, and to discipline and train her up in the Exercises and Spirit of the most difficult and heroick Christian Virtues. Nevertheless, so subtle is the baneful Poison of Self-love, as often to escape the most watchful Eye, and so deeply is it rivetted in the Soul since the Corruption of our Nature by sin, that it is not to be thoroughly expelled without the farther powerful Aid of sharp interiour Trials, which, when supported by a perfect Spirit of Prayer, penetrate and cleanse the innermost Affections of the Soul. The same are also Occasions or Instruments of the most heroick Virtues, inasmuch as they are far more severely felt than outward Afflictions. It therefore happens by a special Disposition of the divine Mercy and Providence, that Souls which God designs to raise to higher Privileges of Grace, usually meet with these firey Trials. Infinitely merciful and infinitely wise is this Dispensation of divine Providence in favour of his Elect; who, by giving

stronger

stronger Proofs of their Fidelity, and by exerting their most vigorous Efforts, grow in Fervour, and are particularly recommended to the divine Favour: and by a Crucifixion of all sensual Appetites, and the Purification of their inward Powers and Faculties, are prepared for the Establishment of the perfect Reign of divine Grace, and to bear the Image of their crucified Redeemer. He was pleased to suffer not only cruel Torments in his Body, but also the most bitter Anguish of Soul in the Garden, and upon the Cross, to expiate the Disorders of our inward Man, and to be our Model in inward Trials, of all others the most severe. On the other Side, the infernal Fiend, who sees a Soul devote herself with Fervour to the divine Service, and dreads her spirit of Humility, Mortification and Prayer, assaults her with the utmost Rage which Malice can inspire, and leaves nothing unattempted to compass her Ruin, or at least to warp or damp her Resolution, and to traverse the Execution of her holy Desires. God in Mercy, and for the Triumph of his Servants, permits the Devil to try them to a certain Degree, as he did *Job*; nay, God him-

himself. seems sometimes as if he were leagued against his own faithful Servant, in raising up Persecutors against her, in leaving her Intellect in Darkness, abandoning her Mind and Imagination to Distractions, and suffering them to be filled with frightful Images, haunted by Objects of Horror and Abomination, and miserably perplexed with vain Fears and Alarms, and troublesome importunate Temptations, depriving her Will of all sensible Relish of Devotion, and alarming it with unspeakable Horrors: in a Word, afflicting all her inward Powers in a Manner not to be expressed, nor even understood by any who have not learned it by their own Experience of that State (39). This his Conduct seems full of Rigour, but it is in Reality an Effect of infinite Mercy and Goodness. He knows our Necessities and the Depth of our Wounds, and he adapts and proportions the Remedy. He knows the Value he has stamped upon the Cross, the Advantages to be reaped by us from it

(39) See St. *Teresa* in her own Life, c. 30, and Mansion 6, St. *John* of the Cross, in his *Obscure Night*, and his *Ascent of Mount Carmel*, *Hilton*, *Harphius*, &c.

it, and the Crown and Trophies which it brings. Nor will he suffer our Trials or Temptations to exceed our Strength, but is ready by his omnipotent Grace to conquer in us and for us. Comforting a Soul in this State, he addresses her in these tender Words (40): *O poor little one, tossed with the Tempest, without all Comfort, behold I will lay thy Stones in Order, and will lay thy Foundations with Sapphires.* And by the Psalmist (41): *Though you sleep in the Midst of extreme Dangers, and seem on the very Brink of Ruin, you shall come forth with Glory and Joy, as a Dove with Wings bright, and of a Silver white, tipped with Gold.* Though the Issue be so happy and so glorious, the first Shock of the Combat is rough. Even those who have sheltered themselves in a religious Retirement from all the outward Storms which worldly Concerns never fail to raise, are not to flatter themselves that the Crown of Virtue is to cost them nothing. It is always a Land of Conquest, not to be taken but by Violence: It is a Mountain reaching to the highest Heaven, even to God himself. The Road is

---

(40) *Isa.* liv. 11.   (41) Pf. lxvii. 14.

is every where crossed by numberless Bypaths, which lead some to one Precipice, others to another. It is not be held without constant Watchfulness, great Resolution, Steadiness and Courage. Indeed God himself is the Light, Strength, and Comfort of those that walk with this Fidelity: yet to try their Constancy he often withdraws for a Time the Ray of his Light, and the Dew of his sweet Comfort. Virtue costs nothing when the Unction of the Holy Ghost accompanies all its Exercises: it is well paid even in this Life, and as it were in Hand, for the Pains that are taken for it. But it is far otherwise when every Thing is Darkness, and attended with Difficulties and heavy Repugnance. Then, however, it is often most perfect and most pleasing to God. We do little for a Friend if we serve him in something which brings us Advantage and Pleasure. But if it be difficult and expensive, then we shew that we do it for his Sake. In like Manner if our Fervour and Zeal carry us with Fidelity through the Deserts and Thorns of a State of a spiritual Dryness, our Love of God will be approved sincere, and grow daily more refined

fined and more perfect. The greatest Saints suffered such Trials; and these were usually a chief Means of raising them through the divine Grace to that eminent Purity of Affections, and Sanctity of Life, which we so much admire in them. In a State of Life which is purely contemplative, and more removed from exteriour Crosses and Afflictions, these interiour Trials, by the special Appointment of divine Providence, seem more frequent and more severe. Sister *Mary* had her Share in bearing this inward Cross.

Some Time after her religious Profession, from a State of spiritual Light and heavenly Consolation she fell into a grievous spiritual Dryness, in which nothing warmed her Affections, no Feelings of Devotion sweetened her Austerities; her Soul was overwhelmed with Darkness, and her Heart was a Stranger to the least Spark of divine Comfort. Had she here fallen into Discouragement or Impatience, had she suffered herself to be drawn from Assiduity in Prayer, or from the penitential Life in which God had called her to walk, to seek Comfort in Creatures, in vain Amusements

Her interiour Trials.

ments, in idle or secular Conversation; or had she laid aside, or grown indifferent, or cold in her religious Exercises, she would by such an Infidelity have deprived herself of the great Graces which God had prepared for her. But her Fidelity and Perseverance shewed her Sacrifice to be generous and heroick, and rendered it perfect and acceptable to God.

A State of spiritual Dryness is a heavy Cross, but in the progress of an interiour spiritual Life much severer Trials lie still behind, and by these was Sister *Mary* to complete her Martyrdom. The Dryness she experienced in her Devotions and other Duties was unutterably aggravated by a most frightful spiritual Darkness, Desolation of Soul, anxious Trouble, alarming Fears and Scrupulosity, and inexpressible Horrors, which Affliction continued for the Space of two whole Years, and was much increased by the Unskilfulness of a spiritual Director, who should have been her chief Support and Comfort, but who understood nothing of her State. However, she followed his and her Superiour's Advice in Simplicity of Heart, never omitted or grew slack

slack in any of her religious Exercises, strenuously laboured, though always calmly, without Fretfulness or Impatience, to resist and put by all importunate Temptations, and to bear up against all desponding Suggestions, with an entire Confidence in the divine Goodness, and Resignation and Sacrifice of herself to God, and to his adorable Will. Her Heart she scarce thought in her own Power, so much it seemed possessed by infernal Fiends. She no longer felt any sweet Inclination toward her sovereign Good, in the Exercises of divine Love: her Mind was so stupid and dull, and so strangely led away by wandering troublesome Thoughts, and alarming Phantoms, that she was scarce able to fix her Attention on God, unless she took some Book into her Hands; nor could she read without continual Distractions. Anger, Impatience, and other Passions, which she lately checked and governed with Ease, were now rouzed, and made furious Assaults, which it was no small Trouble to watch against and restrain. So far was she removed from the late happy State in which her Soul was full of Light, Sweetness, Fervour, and generous

rous Courage, that no Traces thereof seemed to remain in her: she even feared lest it might not have been an Illusion of the Enemy. She saw nothing in herself but Darkness, and felt nothing but Coldness, Wretchedness, and cruel Sadness, with which she was quite overwhelmed. All this Time she ceased not to lament her past Sins and Abuse of Grace, to which she imputed this Chastisement: she adored the Hand of God, acquiesced in his Will, and offered herself to suffer whatever Severities he should be pleased to treat her with: and with many Tears implored his Mercy, and the Grace of his holy Love. The very Shadow of Sufferings which were formerly her Joy, now alarmed and terrified her. Yet she bore her heavy Cross with Constancy and Submission, under which she sought no Relief but in Obedience, the Sacraments, pious Books and Prayer, which nevertheless afforded her no sensible Comfort. She seemed to walk on the Brink of the most frightful Precipices, in Danger every Moment of falling into the Gulph of that false Humility, of which B. *Angela*, of *Fulgineo*, draws a just and horrible

ble Portraiture (42), or of Vain-glory and Pride: of Pusillanimity, Despondency and Despair: of spiritual Sloth, Lukewarmness, and Indifference: or of abandoning her Exercises and seeking Comfort in Creatures. Amidst these Precipices God held his Servant by the Hand, supported her, and conducted her safe. In the Strength of his Almighty Arm she walked without Hurt over the Aspick and the Basilisk, and trampled on the Lion and Dragon (43). A Soul in such a State seems to herself to be doing nothing, and fears that even her Prayers are an Abomination before God, that she is abandoned by him, and wandering from the Path of true Virtue. But if she stedfastly cleaves to God, she then advances most toward him by learning sincerely to enter into a deep Sense of her own Nothingness, spiritual Poverty, Nakedness, and absolute Unworthiness, and to have no Reliance but on God alone. He by this seeming Rigour completes the great Work of the Crucifixion of the Old Man in her, and cleanses all her Affections and Powers, in order to

(42) In her own Life, or Theology of the Cross, b. 2. part 1. c. 5. (43) Ps. xc. 13.

to open to her all the Treasures of his Grace, to take entire Possession of her Heart, and fill it with himself alone. And he never is more powerfully with her than whilst he seems in this State to have most abandoned her; then it is that he most visibly covers her with the Shield of his omnipotent Presence, and gives her that Strength by which, like another *Job*, she foils the Enemy in all his Assaults, and triumphs over the Powers of Hell.

Mary in this State suffered a true inward Martyrdom. Almighty God, who all this Time fought in her, and with her, beheld her Conflicts with singular Complacency, and in his tender Bowels of infinite Love and Mercy, waited the Term to put an End to this severe Probation, that he might display his Goodness in her in such a Manner as to compensate the apparent Rigour of his long Absence by sweeter Caresses, and more sensible Evidences of his Love. At length her Fears, and that Darkness which clouded her Understanding, were dispelled: she found a bright Gleam of heavenly Light on a sudden break in upon her Soul, and from that Moment
she

she was restored to her former Peace and holy Joy. She then began to enlarge her Affections in divine Love, Thanksgiving, Praise, and Compunction, with an Ardour and ravishing Sweetness, far beyond what she had ever before experienced. Then it appeared by her profound Humility, unalterable Meekness, and the Fervour of her Charity and Devotion; how surprising a Change the divine Grace had wrought in her, and what a Progress she had made in all Virtues by these Trials. From the entire Annihilation of herself, and the most intimate Sense of her own Wretchedness, Poverty and Weakness, and her most enlarged feeling Conceptions of God's boundless Goodness, Mercy, Sanctity, Love, Immensity, and other Attributes, she was so grown in all spiritual Science as to have attained to the Lights of the Saints. This twofold Knowledge of God and herself taught her to penetrate with the most feeling Sentiments of Devotion into the unfathomed Abyss of the Mysteries of the divine Mercy, and of our holy Religion, and to contemplate them with Raptures of unutterable Fervour, in Adoration, Compunction, Love, and
Thanks-

Thanksgiving, with the entire Sacrifice of herself to God, through our divine Redeemer, and to live in the closest Union of her Soul with him, enriching herself more and more by the Communication of his Graces, and drawing his Image more and more perfect in her Soul by the Transcript of all Virtues from their great Original, and the Source of all Graces. This spiritual experimental Knowledge, and lively active Faith was in her the Root or Foundation of a perfect Spirit of Humility, Meekness, Hope, Love, and all other Virtues; and in the first Place of an extraordinary Gift or Spirit of Prayer.

Her eminent Spirit of Prayer, and its Advantages.

A Spirit of Prayer is the eldest Daughter of divine Love, or a principal Fruit which that divine Seed produces in us. It is the proper Employ of his Love, its Nourishment, Comfort, and Support: Nay of actual divine Love it may be called the vital Action or Exercise; in it we glorify God by our most perfect Homages, and by the Tribute of our Affections, and all our Powers, and are reciprocally glorified and enriched by him, who through the Channel of holy Prayer

Prayer bestows on us all the Treasures of his Grace, and raises us even to a close Union with himself, whilst the Soul annihilates herself before him, and enlarges her Affections in Acts of Adoration, Thanksgiving, Praise, Love, Compunction, and Supplication, laying open her spiritual Miseries and Necessities to him, and with *unutterable Sighs* imploring his Mercy; he on his Side visits her with infinite Tenderness and Bounty, dispels the Darkness of her Understanding by the bright Rays of his heavenly Light, in which he teaches her to penetrate, and form enlarged Conceptions of the great Truths of his holy Scriptures, of our divine Faith, and of the incomprehensible Mysteries of his Love, Mercy, and Justice, also of all the Theological and Moral Virtues, and their Motives, &c. In a Word, he experimentally instructs her in a feeling Knowledge of herself, her Sinfulness and Miseries, and of Him, her sovereign Good and last End. At the same Time he purifies and fills her Imagination and Memory with pure and holy Images, and inflames her Will with the strongest heavenly Desires and Affections, and replenishes her with chaste Delights and Joy.

Joy. Thus heavenly Contemplation takes its Rise from divine Love, being its Daughter and its Exercise, as St. *Thomas Aquinas* observes (1): For Love moves the Soul to fix her Eyes on her Beloved, by desiring to behold, contemplate, and glorify him. Again by contemplating him with Admiration, Joy, and Love, invited by his Goodness and other infinitely adorable and amiable Perfections she is inflamed with more ardent Love, from which again her Knowledge of God is more and more enlarged, and the Light of her Understanding much increased. Hence in Contemplation, and in all devout Prayer, the Powers of the Soul move, and mutually assist each other in a wonderful Kind of Circle. For the Will by Love is the first Spring in Contemplation, and this, which is an Action of the Understanding, kindles afresh, and more vehemently the Fire of Love in the Will, which again casts brighter and clearer Rays of divine Light and Knowledge upon the Understanding. With divine Love all other Virtues are here strengthened, improved, and perfected. Faith becomes lively and

(1) St. *Tho.* 2. 2. qu. 180. a. 1.

and vigorous; Hope invincible; Penance and Mortification are stirred up to cut off and expiate all Offences; Temperance to subdue and govern all the Appetites and Passions: Humility in the first Place to purge away all the subtle Leaven of Pride: these and all other Virtues to exert themselves in all heroick Actions, with incredible Ardour and Courage, which feels no Labour or Difficulties (2).

This Spirit of Grace and Prayer (3), the admirable Key of all heavenly Treasures and Graces, and the great Teacher of divine Love, was promised by the Prophets to be poured forth with unbounded Profusion in the new Law of Grace and Love (4), in which all the Children of the Church are to be *taught of God*. By it in the primitive Ages so many great Pastors so many devout Monks and Hermits, so many Saints in every Station amidst the World, all eminently Men of Prayer, appeared like Angels on Earth to sanctify it. How comes it that in these later Ages this hea-

(2) *Isa.* lii. 11.   (3) *Zach.* xii. 10.
(4) Ib. and *John* vi. 45. 1. *John*, ii. 27. *John*, 4. 23.

heavenly Grace is so sparingly bestowed that scarce are any Traces of it to be found. Even in those holy States of Life in which Men are sequestered from the World, in Order to devote themselves to the holy Exercises of Penance and Prayer, whether in the publick Ministry of the Church, or in the retired Sanctuaries of Recluses, where shall we find the true Heirs of this Spirit? Do not Christians in general seem now-a-days even Strangers to it? So little are many acquainted with it as to seem to suspect its very Name or Definition, which is to them a strange Language. Nevertheless, let chaste Souls which burn with holy Zeal for the divine Honour, be comforted amidst so frightful a Contagion, so general a Desolation, God, ever faithful to his Word, raises up continually in the sacred Sanctuary of his Church, many holy terrestrial Angels, by whom his Name will be to the End of Time glorified on Earth, and the Church militant ever joined with the triumphant in paying him incessant pure Homages of Adoration, Thanksgiving, Praise, Compunction and Love: *Adorers in Spirit and Truth*. Their Number indeed is exceeding

ing small, and as St. *Austin* pathetically complains, so small, and often their Life so perfectly hidden in Christ, as not to appear discernible in the World, in Comparison of the great Number of those who are sunk, in different Degrees, under a carnal Spirit, or at least fettered by the unhappy Ties of Self-love, and blinded by its false Illusions. But though these true and perfect Servants of God are few in comparison of those, who walk not in this Path, they will be found to make a great and glorious Assembly at the last Day, when united in the Company of the heavenly Spirits. Even now on Earth they form continually in the Church a happy Society of Saints, glorious and acceptable in the Sight of Heaven; and by them a Tribute of holy Praise is sent up as a sweet Incense from Earth to the Throne of God (5).

After all, can we wonder that an infused special Gift of Prayer, though by the divine Mercy it is offered to all, should be so rare a Privilege? It is a Property, or the Offspring of perfect Charity, which can only be built upon the Ruins of vanquished Cupidity, or inordinate Self-love,

the

(5) *Isa.* xxiv. 14 16.

the Root of all the irregular Passions of the human Heart.

The Spirit of Prayer is twofold; the one *acquired*, which is an Habit of praying with profound Humility, Confidence, Attention, Earnestness, and Perseverance, acquired by a Preparation of the Soul, holy Attention to God, and repeated fervent Acts of devout Prayer, with the Succour of actual Graces: The other is *infused*, far more excellent and perfect: This, like its Parent, the divine Love from which it springs, is in its very Nature a supernatural Habit, and most gratuitous Gift, infused or communicated by the Holy Ghost. Nevertheless, it requires certain Conditions in the Soul, by which Obstacles are removed, and she is prepared and disposed for the Reception of so great a Grace. The first is a Disengagement of the Soul from Self-love and the World, or a great Purity of Heart. Only *the Clean of Heart shall see God* (6). The second is an ardent Desire of tending to Christian Perfection, conquering all Difficulties, and living *without Reserve* to God alone, or to please him. *The Beginning of Wisdom is the most true Desire of Discipline* (7). She who

(6) *Mat.* v. 8.   (7) *Wisd.* vi. 19.

runs with the most vehement Desires and Earnestness, takes the largest Strides, and arrives the soonest at the Goal, says St. *Bernard* (8). But as the devout *Richard* of *St. Victor* observes (9), this Desire must not be barren, but fruitful and active in the fervent unwearied Exercise of all Virtues. Hence *Cassian* tells us (10), that they labour in vain who aim at the Grace of holy Contemplation without accompanying their Endeavours with the most fervent Exercise of all Virtues. The heavenly Bridegroom invites the beloved Spouse to shew the Sincerity and Constancy of her Love, by her Diligence in adorning her House, and strewing her Bed with the sweetest and most beautiful Flowers (11).

Various are the Gifts of the divine Spirit in holy Prayer, according to that of the Apostle (12). *There are diversities of Graces, but the same Spirit - - - dividing to every one according as he will.* So Christ also said to *Nicodemus: The Spirit breatheth where he will.* But it is a Maxim of great

(8) Serm. 3. de Circumcif. (9) *Richard* a St. *Victore*, l. de Præparat. ad Contemplat. c. 79. (10) *Cassian*, Collat. xiv. 2, and 3. (11) St. *Bernard*, Serm. 46, in Cant. (12) 1 *Cor*. xii. 4. 11. *Joa*. iii. 8.

great Importance, which must be always attended to on this Subject; that, the Excellency and Advantages of Prayer are not to be measured by any sublime or extraordinary Gifts or Degrees in it, but by the Humility, Purity, and Fervour of the divine Love, from which it springs, and the Increase which it gives to the same Love. Hence a fervent and humble Prayer put up in a State of spiritual Dryness, and inward Desolation of Soul may be far more profitable, and a more excellent Homage and Sacrifice to God than the most sublime Degree of passive Prayer. Though indeed this is a precious Grace, and of the highest Advantage in an interiour Life, when faithfully corresponded with in humble Fear and Compunction; yet many eminent Saints have never been called to this Kind of Contemplation. Even a Desire of it, or Self-complacency in it would always be a most dangerous Illusion, and criminal Presumption, teeming with most fatal Mischiefs.

What is meant by Supernatural Prayer. To explain in a few Words what is meant by this Degree of Prayer, we must take Notice, that all Christian Prayer, inas-

inasmuch as it is grounded in Faith, nourished by Hope, and perfected by the Breathings of divine Charity, is necessarily the Fruit of Supernatural Grace, which enlightens, excites, strengthens, and raises the Faculties of the human Mind above their natural Capacity and Power. But a certain Prayer is peculiarly called *Supernatural* and *Passive*, because it excludes all Concurrence of human Industry, being excited by so strong an Influx of the Holy Ghost as forcibly to apply the Understanding and Will to God alone, and to suspend all foreign Action of the Senses, or of external Objects or Creatures upon them. It would be a gross Error to imagine with the *Quietist* Hereticks, that the Powers of the Soul exert no Actions in this State, but are *merely* Passive: For in it the Understanding sees or contemplates great Truths of Faith in the divine Light, and the Will is employed in Acts of Adoration, Admiration, Love, Humiliation, &c. but with so great Ease and Joy that the Soul scarce perceives herself to act, and seems rather to receive Impressions, and to enjoy than herself to act. The most ancient ascetick Writers and Fathers from

the SS. *Clements, Antonies, Macariuses, Climacuses* and *Cassians*, to SS. *Bernard, Thomas Aquinas, Bonaventure, Teresa*, &c. frequently and clearly speak of this passive Prayer, yet without descending to minute Distinctions, such as we find in several modern Mysticks, unnecessary to those who have experienced them, and unintelligible to others. These we are to distinguish from heavenly Gusts and Consolations in ordinary Prayer; Favours which God frequently communicates to many to strengthen their Weakness, and to encourage them in his Love and Service, by a Relish of his Sweetness. Of these the devout Contemplative, *Richard* of *St. Victor* says (13), " The holy Scrip-
" tures call this inward Sweetness some-
" times a *Taste* or *Relish*, because, com-
" pared to the Delights of Heaven, they
" are so small as to be scarce to be called
" Drops from that boundless Fountain:
" and sometimes an *Inebriation*, because
" compared to worldly Pleasures, these
" exceed them beyond all Bounds of
" Comparison." These, which in various Degrees are ordinary and frequent in a spiritual Life, have no immediate Af-

(13) *Rich. a St. Victore*, in *Benjamin Minor*.

Affinity with those Favours which are far more rare and sublime, of passive Prayer. This is chiefly twofold. 1st. The *Prayer of Quiet*, to which belongs the *Prayer of pure Faith*: And, 2dly. The *Prayer of Union*. The first is more the Action of the Intellect, than of the Will, for it is an intellectual Contemplation of God's infinite Perfections, through the Medium of a boundless Ocean of Light, as of something unutterable, invisible, and incomprehensible, only to be conceived by Negatives. The Soul sees Him to be super-eminently and infinitely all Love, all Wisdom, all Power, all Goodness, all Felicity, &c. without attempting insolently to penetrate that Abyss. Hence she discovers herself to be in a State of Ignorance and Darkness in respect to God. Though the Soul be wholly absorpt in this Contemplation, yet the Will has its Part in this Prayer, by Acts of sweet Love, Adoration, Joy, &c. but exerted with so great Ease and Inclination, that the Soul scarce perceives any Exertion of that Power. In the *Prayer of Union*, which is the most sublime Act of passive Contemplation, the Will chiefly is employed by Love, entering the Cloud with *Moses*, and closely uniting itself to,

and

and swallowed up in the immense Ocean of the sovereign increated Good, with an insatiable Desire, and enlarged feeling Knowledge of it, and sweet unspeakable Relish of His Love. In all passive Prayer the other Faculties, viz. the Memory and Imagination, are stilled and suspended; also the Senses, so that the Soul receives no Impression from outward Objects through them. The Gifts of passive Prayer give the Soul a sovereign Contempt and Loathing of the World and its Vanities, and a strong Desire of beholding and ever enjoying God in his Glory, with a firm Hope of that Happiness(14). This may suffice concerning Gifts, which are not the Fruit of human Industry, which cannot be desired or sought without Presumption and gross Illusion, which are not Marks of greater

(14) See on them *Cassian* and other antient Ascetick Fathers. St. *Bernard*, *(Serm. 41. in Cant.)* St. *Bonaventure*, *(Itiner 6. dist. 1. Itin. 5. dist. 6. and De. 7. grad. Contempl.)* *Gerson*, *(Alphab. 86. and de monte Contempl. c. 8.) Dionysius Carthus*, *(in Exod. Art. 42. p. 406. and l. de Fonte Lucis. Art. 14. and Theol. Myst. Art. 9.)* St. *Teresa*, *(her own Life. c. 19. &c. and Mans. 7. c. 1) Harphius*, *(Theol. Mystic. l. 3. c. 23)* S. *Francis* of *Sales*, *(l. On the Love of God.)* or in Abstract, with the greatest Precision. *Thomas* à Jesu, *(De Contemplatione Divina. Octavo.)* and *L' Esprit de la Doctrine de S. Teresa*, Octavo, *Anvers* 1709. *ch.* i. 4. and 7. &c.

greater Sanctity, and ought not to come into Competition with fervent Exercises of Compunction, Penitential Love, &c. The only Reflection necessary on this Subject is, that no one who desires to make any Progress in an interiour Life, should ever suffer himself to be diverted from the Path of assiduous, earnest, and most humble Prayer, in which he will faithfully follow the Call of divine Grace.

To return to our holy Contemplative, though most fervent in the most heroick Practices of Humility, Meekness, Penance, and all other Virtues, she seemed to surpass herself in her ardent Affection for devout Prayer, in all its Branches. This she called with St. *Bernard*, the Business of Businesses, in a Christian Life the most ordinary Instrument of all other Virtues, the chiefest Source of divine Light, Grace, and Comfort; the Novitiate of Heaven, the constant Sacrifice of our Hearts to God, and the Flame and sweet Incense of His Love. Upon the Return of the sensible Visits of the divine Comforter, she was favoured with new and extraordinary Graces, which continually renewed in her Breast, and were reciprocally renewed by the most pure

pure Sighs of divine Love and Compunction. In these burning Desires she often burst into these holy Aspirations, familiar to all loving Souls. *O Lord, if I have found Favour in thy Sight, shew me thy Face, shew me thy Glory* (15). *Shew me, O Thou, whom my Soul loveth; where thou feedest, where thou lyest in the Midday,* in thy meridian Glory (16). *What have I in Heaven? And besides thee what do I desire upon Earth* (17)? *Let him Kiss me with the Kiss of his Mouth* (18). Upon those Aspirations St. *Bernard* in his Comments enlarges as follows: " And what " now remains for me, good Lord, after " having tasted of the Sweetness of thy " Love, but that in the full Brightness " of thy meridian Light, in the Fervour " of Love, I may be graciously admitted " to the Salute of thy Mouth, and filled " with the Joy of thy Countenance (19)." And again: " To be admitted in Spirit " to kiss his Feet, and water them con- " tinually with my Tears, in the Spirit " of Humility and Compunction, ought " to be the Height of my Desires, infi-
" nitely

(15) *Exod.* xxxiii. 13. 18.   (16) Cant. i. 6.
(17) Pf. lxxii. 25.   (18) Cant. i. 1.   (19) Serm. 3 in Cant.

"nitely unworthy as I am. How then
"do I presume to ask a Salute of his
"Mouth. I am not insensible of his
"immense Greatness, and infinite Sanc-
"tity, nor of my own Nothingness and
"Baseness. But I feel the Violence of
"his Love, and I know and experience
"the Excess of his Goodness. The Ve-
"hemence of Love is not to be held
"back; I am not ungrateful for Fa-
"vours received, of the least of which
"I am the most undeserving. But the
"Desire of his Salute suffers me not to
"listen to motives of Awe and Bashful-
"ness. Call it not Presumption, where
"strong Love silences all other Conside-
"rations. The Consciousness of my
"own Baseness cries out to withhold
"me, and check my impetuous De-
"sires; but Love conquers all Obsta-
"cles. I am no Stranger to the sove-
"reign Majesty of the King, and I am
"sensible what Respect and Dread it
"commands: but Love is not to be
"restrained. He, whose very Essence
"is Love and Goodness itself, will listen
"to its Cry. I beg, I supplicate, I in-
"treat: May he salute me with the
"Kiss

" Kiss of his Mouth (20)." Such like burning Aspirations after the Enjoyment of God, and the closest Union of her Soul with him, by sweet Love, the holy Servant of God repeats in all Parts of her manuscript Instructions and Devotions, with singular Tenderness and Ardour; but every where intermixed with the most profound Sentiments of Compunction and Humility.

She was most careful never, if possible, to discover any Thing of extraordinary heavenly Favours received in Prayer, which others might any Way perceive. Much less did she ever desire or ask them of God. In profound Humility she rather cried out with St. *Peter, Depart from me, O Lord, for I am a Sinner.* And with her Patroness, St. *Colette: Lord God, it is enough for me if I know thee, and the Sins which I have committed against thee, that by*

(20) Non sum ingrata, sed amo. Accepi, fateor, meritis potiora sed prorsus inferiora votis: Desiderio feror, non Ratione. Ne quæso causemini Præsumptionem, ubi Affectio urget. Pudor sane reclamat, sed superat Amor. Nec ignoro quod *Honor Regis Judicium diligit;* sed Præceps Amor, nec Judicium præstolatur, nec Consilio Temperatur, nec Pudore frænatur, nec Rationi subjicitur, rogo, supplico, flagito, *Osculetur me osculo oris sui.* Serm. 9. in Cant.

by continual penitential Tears I may obtain of thee Pardon for them. With St. *Teresa,* B. *Angela,* of *Foligni,* and other humble Servants of God, she endeavoured to resist extraordinary Favours of Spiritual Comforts, when able, especially in publick Prayer, and where others were present. This Rule is often inculcated by the most experienced Masters of a spiritual Life; the Venerable *John* of *Avila,* in several Epistles, the Devout *Hilton,* and others. An eminent Penitent and Contemplative explains the Motives as follows (21): " To God it belongeth to
" bestow rare and excellent Gifts, and to
" the Creature to decline and refuse
" them. It is suitable to the divine
" Goodness to draw near to a Soul; and
" it is the Duty of a Soul in Humility
" to draw back, as St. *Peter* did, because
" it is her Duty to humble and abase her-
" self. For, as corrupt Nature seeks in
" all Things Elevation, so our Soul,
" enlightened by Grace, ought incessant-
" ly, and on all Occasions, to embrace
" Poverty and Lowliness, that so she
" may be no less careful and resolute to
" overcome herself, and be upon her
                                    " Guard

(21) Pr. On Interiour Abnegation.

"Guard against the Snares of Pride
"than Self-love is to seek itself. Thus
"there must be a continual Contest be-
"tween God and the humble Soul, ef-
"pecially those Souls which are more
"inclined to aim at sublime Things,
"must necessarily make more Resist-
"ance, and not yield till God so forci-
"bly attracts them, as to take from
"them the Power of withdrawing them-
"selves." The least Self-complacency, or presumptuous Desire in these Matters, destroys in the Heart the true Spirit of Humility and Compunction, the Soul of the interiour Life, and of solid Devotion; and by the Abuse of the divine Grace leads into the most frightful Abyss of Ruin. "I would not have
"that Consolation which taketh from
"me Compunction and the Knowledge
"of myself; nor that Contemplation
"which leads to be high-minded. Every
"high Thing is not holy, nor every
"sweeet Thing good, nor every Desire
"pure, nor every Thing that is dear
"to us pleasing to God. I willingly ac-
"cept that Grace, whereby I may be-
"come more humble, may fear God
"more,

"more, and learn more readily to re-
"nounce myself (22)."

With this essential Precaution, with these Dispositions, the extraordinary Gifts of Grace in Prayer, especially the Prayer of *Union*, are, as was before observed, wonderfully profitable in advancing the perfect Sanctification of a Soul. For though this Prayer be called *Passive*, inasmuch as no one can either dispose himself to it, or procure it, at Pleasure and by his own Endeavours, or always resist and reject this free infused Grace, and its Action is scarce perceptible to the Soul herself; yet we are not to imagine it to be an Inaction; for the Soul in it is employed in the most sublime Acts of Love and Contemplation. By these the Understanding is wonderfully enlightened in the Knowledge of spiritual Things, and the Affections of the Will are purified, strengthened, and inflamed by an unutterable Relish of the same. Here a Soul more perfectly sees and feels her own Nothingness, Miseries, and Baseness, and on the other Side is most feelingly penetrated with a Sense of God's spotless Sanctity, and infinite

Wis-

(22) Imit. b. ii. ch. 10.

Wisdom, Goodness and Majesty; and hereby is exceedingly advanced in perfect Humility and divine Love. In this heavenly Light and Grace many most subtle Defects and secret Stains of her Affections and Actions are discovered and perfectly removed, as the smallest Motes become visible by being placed in the strong Light of the Sun-beams. Hence from a single Act of this Prayer, an Habit remains ingrafted in the Soul of forming more pure and fervent Aspirations and Prayers, and the Imagination and other Powers of the Soul are more perfectly subdued, and more easy and habitually governed and restrained by a sweet and easy Recollection and Tendency to heavenly Things. In a Word, Meekness and all other interiour Virtues are hence exceedingly perfected, so that an experienced Master assures us, that many Years spent in Mortification and other Exercises of Prayer, do not usually so much purify and reform the Heart and Affections, as this Grace in a few Minutes.

This is not to be understood as if Prayer alone could have this wonderful Effect. It must be founded in a sincere
Spi-

Spirit of Humility, Compunction, and holy Love, and accompanied with an habitual Practice of Self-denial, and all Virtues. Without this Condition the true Spirit, and all other neceſſary Conditions of Prayer, are ſo far wanting that it will be rather a Lip-ſervice than an Homage of the Heart. Thus ſome after ſpending the whole Morning in the Church, come home more peeviſh, proud, and froward, than at other Times, to the Scandal of Devotion, which they abuſe. Such live continually Slaves to Self-love and various Paſſions, a Diſgrace to Religion, which they practice ill, and Strangers to the admirable Advantages and Sweetneſs of holy Prayer, and unacquainted with an interiour Life. The Stench of that Corruption which their Heart exhales, buried under the Dunghill of their vicious Appetites, drives away the Holy Ghoſt, or at leaſt compels him to withhold his precious Gifts, and eſpecially his excellent Spirit of Prayer. What Wonder if ſuch who miſtake the very Nature of Prayer, place it in the Multitude of their Words, and meaſure it by the Hours they employ in it; never learn in what this divine Art conſiſts, and

and never reap any Share in the wonderful Fruits it produces in *the Man of Desires*, in the Soul which pours forth itself *in the Spirit of Grace and Prayer*, with *unutterable Groanings*, which the Holy Ghost himself excites in her. So remarkable are these Effects of holy Prayer, that a truly devout Person returning from conversing humbly with God in this heavenly Exercise, seems to bear the Marks of his divine Presence in his very Countenance, and whole meek and heavenly Demeanor, breathing an angelical Spirit of divine Love, Humility, Patience, Compunction, and all Virtues, as *Moses* descending from the Mountain on which he had conversed with God, carried on his Forehead Marks of his Glory, but much more bore the divine Image (by an Imitation of his Virtues and Spirit) strongly impressed on his Soul. This happy inward spiritual Transformation of the Soul is so extraordinary and sensible after the perfect Union of her Powers with God, in the Degrees of Passive Prayer, especially *that of Union*, as to appear often miraculous.

Of this the Life of our holy Servant of God was a wonderful Instance. Others
re-

remarked in her that a new extraordinary Improvement in an angelical Spirit and Temper of Mind, was a visible Proof to them that she had been favoured with a particular Visit of the divine Spirit, whose Presence is the Sanctification of Souls. These Favours, however, had Alternatives. The most spiritual Life is chequered from Time to Time with a Substraction of sensible Graces, and with frequent severe Trials for the Exercise of Patience and other heroick Virtues, by which Heaven is to be purchased, and God is principally glorified by us in this Mortal Life. If when the Dew of heavenly Consolations fattens the dry Land of the Heart, Flowers of all Virtues spring up, by which the Soul is made every Day more acceptable to God, and a Paradise of Delights in which he is pleased to make his Abode; in the Season of spiritual Dryness all interiour Virtues are more heroick, and often more pleasing to God, more Pure, and of sweeter Odour. The Soul thus in both States continually advances towards God with such constant Fidelity, and in all virtuous Exercises, that nothing stays her in her Progress in a spiritual Life.

In

In perfect Submission to God she ever offers herself an entire Sacrifice to him, in holy inward Peace, and finds every where particular Occasions of heroick Virtue, and receives special Graces, all which she improves to her more perfect Sanctification. Many are deceived by the subtle Stratagems of the Enemy, who persuades them under Trials of spiritual Aridity, to lay aside Part of their Exercises of Piety, and out of Indulgence to their Infirmities, to seek Comfort too eagerly in Creatures, or dissipating worldly Amusements. By listening to such dangerous Temptations, they have suffered themselves to be drawn aside from the Path of an interiour Life, and sometimes forfeited their Crown.

Sister *Mary* of the Cross, by her constant Fidelity to God, and her singular Love of the Ways of Humiliation and the Cross, was secured from these Dangers, and made daily Progress in Humility and the Contempt of herself, and in the Purity and Fervour of her Love, and Intention with which in every Action she dedicated herself a perpetual Victim to God, in the most perfect Sacrifice of Fidelity, Submission, Obedience, and Love.

Love. If ever the Heavens seemed of Brass to her, so that no Ray of divine Light penetrated her Understanding, no Dew of heavenly Unction or Comfort softened her heart; she, nevertheless, looking upon herself as a Beast of Burden, with the same constant Zeal and Exactitude, was the first, and most fervent in every Duty, especially of Prayer. Those who at the due Hour think themselves indisposed for that heavenly Exercise, or who, on other like Pretences, easily defer it, are sure to find themselves less disposed afterward, and so fall into a State of frightful Remissness and Disorder. Spiritual Sloth fostered and strengthened by such a Conduct, entirely enervates the Vigour of the Soul in all spiritual Exercises, disqualifies her for corresponding with the divine Graces, and obliges God to withdraw his bountiful Hand. Sister *Mary* considered herself in every Duty called upon to wait on her Creator, and make him a Tender of the Homages which his Creatures are bound to pay him on so many essential Titles. To be dilatory or backward on so solemn, so awful Occasions, would have seemed a Crime and a Baseness, of which a Servant

vant of God on Earth, ought to be as incapable by voluntary Remissness, as an Angel who assists before the Throne of God, in Heaven. Our young Religious burning with holy Zeal to glorify Him continually, she could never listen to any Suggestions of pretended Impediments, so as wilfully to fail in the least Moment of Time, or any other Circumstance. Her extraordinary Assiduity and Devotion in the divine Office, recommended her to the Community, and having also an excellent and most agreeable Voice for the Choir, she was chosen Mistress of the Choir, whilst yet very young. This Office she discharged with the Zeal and Piety of a terrestrial Seraph, and so endeavoured to direct and animate the whole Choir, as to make it a Copy or Imitation of that of the heavenly Spirits, who always assist before the Throne of the most High. An Emulation of their Purity, Zeal, and Devotion, appeared in the Countenance, Voice, and whole Deportment of the Virgin Chorister.

Some Time after she was chosen second, and afterward first Portress, by which Office she was charged with the Dispatch of Business with Persons without

out Doors, with entertaining Strangers, and the Detail of the Accounts, and the Management of the temporal Affairs of the whole Community, as with buying and providing all Neceffaries, paying the Bills of Tradefmen, &c. This Office is of the utmoſt Importance for both the temporal and ſpiritual Welfare of the whole Houſe, and ufually of all others the moſt dangerous, by the continual Occaſions to which it expoſes a religious Perſon, of converſing too much at the Grate, and there contracting the Spirit of the World, of Vanity and Diffipation, the Poiſon and Death of a religious Spirit. The conſtant Recollection of her Soul in God, her Attention to anſwer every Call, as if it had been the Voice of Heaven; her invincible Meekneſs, tender Charity and Sweetneſs toward all, her punctual Exactneſs in every Duty, and her Prudence in dexterouſly avoiding all ſuperfluous or idle Converſation, ſhewed how deep Root every religious Virtue had taken in her Heart, and how eaſy and familiar its moſt heroick and perfect Practice was to her. By her Vigilance the Monaſtery was inacceffible to the Slanders, Detractions, Jealouſies, Feuds,

H 2 and

and all Discourse of Pride, Vanity, Avarice, and other Passions which infect the World, form its Spirit, and chiefly make up its Conversation: and which by idle gossipping Visitants too easily penetrate the closest Sanctuaries of religious Houses. Humility, Charity, holy Zeal, Piety, and all Christian Virtues, seasoned and animated all the Discourse that was held at this Grate, and an heavenly Fire was kindled in the Hearts of those who approached it. A decent Liberty, Cheerfulness, and seasonable Facetiousness preserved their Rights: Yet were mixed with a religious Gravity, and such a Spirit of heavenly Virtue presided in the Conversation, and regulated every one's Words and Behaviour, as could not fail exceedingly to edify all that were present. Moreover, the pious Words of Instruction and Advice which were frequently and appositely thrown out, strongly incited many to the ardent Love of God, and perfect Virtue. Her Words were always few, and confined to the necessary purposes of Charity, where God was not the Subject; and an Attention to his holy Presence, and the Practice of frequent Aspirations, made even

even the Speak-houſe a Houſe of Prayer. Such a Virtue recommended the devout Portreſs to the whole Community, and notwithſtanding her cloſe Retirement and Secreſy, became the Admiration of all who frequented the Monaſtery. God was at length pleaſed to call her forth to the Office of Abbeſs, or Superiour of the Monaſtery, that ſhe might miniſter Comfort, and be a Means of Sanctification to many, reſtore a perfect religious Spirit and Diſcipline, and be a Directreſs of a numerous Community, in the true Path of Chriſtian Perfection.

In the Year 1702, Mother *Giffard*, the Abbeſs, though a very virtuous Superiour, was deposed, and Mr. *Govey*, great Vicar, and ordinary Superiour of the *Engliſh* Monaſtery at *Roüen*, came to the Houſe by an Order of the Archbiſhop, on the 22d of *December*, in the Afternoon, to prepare the Nuns to proceed to the Election of an Abbeſs the next Morning. On this Occaſion he made them a very inſtructive Exhortation. That Night the Bleſſed Sacrament was expoſed in the Church, and ſeveral of the Nuns ſpent almoſt the whole Night in Prayer to recommend

She is choſen Abbeſs.

commend the Affair to God. The next Morning Mr. *Govey* went again to the Nunnery, and having said the Conventual Mass, in which he gave the Communion to all the Nuns, came up to the Grate of the Choir to open the Election, being attended by two Witnesses, who were the Confessarius and Mr. *Cary*. The Nuns went to the Grate one by one to give their Votes in writing, which they put into a little Dish, set for that Purpose, none of the Nuns being allowed to know the Vote of any of her Sisters; it is even strictly forbid for them ever to mention it to one another, either before or after the Election. Two-thirds of the Voices being required for a Canonical Election of Abbess; the great Vicar, after taking out the Votes, and shewing them to the two Witnesses, declared Sister *Mary* of the Holy Cross canonically chosen by forty-two Voices. The late Abbess had Six, and others some, but not enough in all to hinder the Election: and it is not to be expressed what Joy and Satisfaction it gave the whole Community to see they had a spiritual Mother and Superiour, who was of so sweet a Character, so experienced in an Interiour Life, and endowed

dowed in so eminent a Degree with Discretion and Sanctity. Only she herself was overwhelmed with Grief and Apprehension, from a lively Sense of the evident Dangers to which Superiority exposes those who are not qualified for the Charge which they undertake, for which, out of profound Humility, she thought herself, of all Persons, the most unfit. She had no sooner heard her Name mentioned by the great Vicar, but she slipt secretly out of the Choir, and went with great Speed into a little Hermitage, in the Scholars Garret, where she remained hid about half an Hour, weeping most bitterly. Great Search was made for her all the House over, and she was at last found in the abovementioned Place, at her Prayers, but in such a Condition, through Fright and Confusion, that she seemed rather dead than alive. They desired her instantly to come down, which she refused to do, alledging that she desired first to speak to the Vicar in the Confession-house: for she always hoped that by laying her Incapacity before him she should persuade him to proceed to another Election. The Vicar sent her Word, that he earnestly desired and intreated her to come; and seeing this did not prevail, he sent her a Command in Virtue of holy Obedience, to make her Appearance. She was then brought between two Sisters up to the Grate, all bathed in Tears. The great Vicar confirmed her Abbess, in the Name of my Lord Archbishop, and commanded all the Nuns to obey her. He could scarce read the Prayers for Weeping, at the Sight of the excessive Grief and Affliction with which she was oppressed, though he comforted her in the best Manner he was able. Then *Te Deum* was sung; after which the late Abbess cordially embraced her, promising to assist her in all she was able. Next all the other Nuns with great Joy did the same, she lying all the while in the Arms of the late Abbess, all drowned in Tears, and overwhelmed with Grief and Apprehension, so that in the End they were forced to conduct her to her Cell, where she was laid upon her Bed. The next Day, which was *Christmas-Eve*, she officiated at Matins, and seeing it was evidently the Will of God, humbly bowed her Shoulders to the heavy Burden, saying, that she looked upon it as laid upon her in Punishment of her Sins. The Archbishop

bishop of *Roüen* wrote her the following Letter soon after her Election.

"I am overjoyed, dear Sister, at your Election. It is what I have long desired, from the Knowledge I have of your Virtue and Prudence: I am entirely persuaded that all the Nuns will be re-united under your Government: I exhort them to follow your Sentiments in all Things, and I desire you to tell them so from me: You may assure yourself that I will support you in every Thing you shall think fit to do for the good Order and Sanctification of your Community: Mr. *Govey* shall continue to take Care of your House as before. I recommend myself to your good Prayers, and those of your Community, and I am with a very particular Esteem,

"my dear Sister,

"entirely your's,

"The Archbishop of *Roüen*."

The Charge of Abbess in this Monastery is for Life, unless some extraordinary Accident obliges the Archbishop to order it otherwise. But Mother *Mary* of the Cross, two Years after her Election, took

Occasion from the Election of the other Officers of the Monastery, to desire earnestly to put herself again to the Votes of the Community, in hopes the Choice might fall upon some other Person. But the great Vicar would not hear of it. Some Years after she attempted again the same Thing, in hopes of being released from her heavy Charge. But all the Community unanimously intreated the great Vicar, who was their Superiour, not to give Ear to her Request, which he assured them he never would do. Indeed all who knew the Monastery exceedingly congratulated with it for the Happiness of having so prudent and holy a Mother Superiour.

She gave her whole Attention to the spiritual Advancement and Perfection of the Community, and that she might be at Liberty to employ her Thoughts and Time in this alone, and in labouring to sanctify her own Soul, she left the entire Management of Temporals to another Sister. Though she never failed to afford her Sisters all spiritual Comfort and Direction, yet she taught them still much more by her Example than by Words. Her Zeal for the most exact Regularity, made her even under her Infirmities force herself

be-

beyond her Strength to be always the firſt in the Choir, and to take Care that all came before the Beginning of Prayer. If any one ſtaid a Moment after the firſt Toll of the Bell, ſhe never let it paſs without a ſevere Reprimand: the leaſt Fault could not eſcape her Vigilance. Her Reprehenſions were made with the neceſſary Authority of a Superiour, but mixed with ſo much Sweetneſs, Charity, and Compaſſion for Human Weakneſs, as took off every Thing that could ſeem harſh to Nature, and clearly ſhewed that ſhe had nothing in View but the Good of Souls, and that no Paſſion had the leaſt Share in what ſhe ſaid or did. All her Corrections were exempt from the leaſt Shadow of Imperiouſneſs. So long as ſhe lived ſhe kept up regular Obſervance and religious Diſcipline in the moſt perfect Vigour, by theſe her conſtant charitable Admonitions. She frequently reproved her Siſters for the leaſt Sloth or Failure, exhorting them continually to the utmoſt Exactitude in all Cuſtoms of the Rule, and in all Ceremonies, particularly of the Choir, to which ſhe had a conſtant Attention. She was of ſo tender a Conſtitution, that whilſt ſhe was a young Nun, her Superiours

ours thought proper not to employ her in any very hard Work, as in Washing, and the like. But when she came to be Superiour she shewed the great Love she had always had for Humiliations, and the hardest and most penitential Labours; for in these she always claimed the greatest Share for her own Part. She was always first at carrying Wood, and such like Work, which she performed with the greatest Cheerfulness, often saying, " Dear Children, this is our Harvest; " let us make our Profit of it." She was most rigid and austere to herself, and whilst she had her Health, would never admit of any Dispensation or Indulgence, and never allowed herself the least corporal Refreshment beyond the Rule, saying sometimes, when others importuned her to use some Mitigation for the Sake of her Health: " There is no Salvation " for Superiours, unless they have Reso- " lution." Under the most violent Fits of the Gravel and Stone, with other Distempers, from which she suffered much, with unspeakable Patience, for several Years before her Death, she would never admit of any Thing to support or comfort her, which was not common to the other

other Sick, and would frequently oblige the Infirmarian to serve her the last, that she might not be preferred. But her Tenderness and Charity for her Sisters, exceeded what could be imagined in her constant Attention to them under their Work, and on all Occasions. The youngest and last in the House found equal Relief from her charitable Compassion, and her Love for every one of them seemed such, as if she had but that one under her Care. Her Sweetness and Affability toward all was equal, and constant on all Occasions. Whenever she saw any of her spiritual Children under any exteriour or interiour Trouble, she presently informed herself of the Cause, and endeavoured to apply a Remedy, at least by suitable Advice and comfortable Instructions. She would ask Advice of the youngest in the House, but would not suffer them to give their Opinion, unless she asked them. Her Contempt of herself was admirable. All the Faults of any in the Community she ascribed to herself, and when she saw any one not do so well as she desired, she would say:
" Alas! the Tree is known by its Fruits.
" You see what poor Fruit I produce.
" The

"The Fault is certainly mine." If at any Time she thought she had given the least Occasion of Offence to any one, though by their not having understood her, she failed not to ask Pardon, even of the Lay-sisters. Her extraordinary Tenderness and Compassion for all that were under her Care, induced every one with Confidence to have Recourse to her in all their Necessities, corporal or spiritual, and she never let any one go away without some Relief. The Sick were always the first Object of her Care, and it was her Study to afford or procure them every Kind of Comfort and Assistance. She often visited them, sat long by them, and put into their Mouths most fervent Aspirations, exciting them to call for Mercy by the sacred Passion and precious Blood of our Saviour; and when they were weary, or unable to attend to, or repeat such Ejaculations, saying them secretly herself for them. It happened once that a poor Sister had a terrible Cancer in her Leg; the charitable Abbess would not trust the Dressing of it to any other, but did it every Day as soon as she was up, and whilst she was fasting, though the Stench was offensive beyond what can be

ima-

imagined. Some reprefented to her that the Infection might be dangerous, and that fhe ought not to expofe herfelf by doing that Office, at leaft, conftantly. But fhe replied, that fhe muft overcome her own Nicenefs, and could not be prevailed upon to defift, till the Sifter died. When others feemed near Death, her Charity for them, in like Manner, was indefatigable, and fhe could no longer be drawn from their Bed-fide, unlefs compelled to it by frequent Importunities, to take fome little Refrefhment. The Poor alfo found in her a true Comforter and Inftructor, and as far as her Poverty would permit her, a fure Refuge for their Relief. She never refted Night or Day till fhe found fhe could be of Service to them; fhe prayed moft ardently for and with them, and would often fay: " Run " to the Paffion of our dear Redeemer, " and to his holy Virgin Mother." Her Words diftilled a Balm of Comfort into the Hearts of all that were in Trouble. This Art fhe had learned from her Meditations on the Sufferings of Chrift, and from her own fevere Trials, efpecially one which fhe bore for two Years, under moft troublefome Difficulties, by which
God

God was pleased to prove her, like Gold in the Furnace, that she might know how to compassionate and instruct others. Perfect Simplicity of Heart rendered her just and upright in all her Conduct, without the least Disguise or Duplicity in Words or Action, of which she had always the utmost Abhorrence: for true Virtue inspires a great Love of Sincerity, even in the least Things, and God being the sovereign Truth, all Hypocrisy or Deceit is an Abomination to him. She had a wonderful Greatness of Soul above her Sex, joined with a profound Humility, which appeared in all her Actions. By the great Tranquility of Soul, which she preserved in the most mortifying and unexpected Events, and in the severest Contradictions, it appeared how perfect an interiour Peace she enjoyed, and how much she was Mistress of her Passions, and raised above all earthly Things, with a strong Faith in God, and an entire Reliance on his Providence for rectifying all Things, when a reasonable Care was taken. On such Occasions she always repeated these Words, "The Will of God." She was endowed with a noble Generosity, and had a great Love and Esteem for religious

religious Poverty, to which she frequently exhorted her spiritual Daughters, calling it the Badge and Spirit of their holy Order. The Advantages of a total Disengagement from, and Privation of, earthly Goods, and worldly Conveniences, she often spoke of with great Feeling: and much more frequently on the Poverty and Nakedness in which our blessed Redeemer for our Sakes was born, lived and died. Her Disinterestedness was entire, she never refused to receive a Postulant for Want of Fortune, or any temporal Consideration, when she seemed truly called to that State, telling her Community, that divine Providence would never fail them, if they were but faithful in their Duties. Her Esteem for holy Obedience was extraordinary, and this Virtue she inculcated to all her spiritual Children, as the Soul of a religious State. Hence, she would never suffer any to affect the least Singularity in their Practices. If any such Thing came to her Knowledge, she gave the Person, who had fallen into it, sharp Rebukes, both in Private and Publick, till such Time that she saw this pernicious Evil was entirely destroyed. And she would say to her who had been drawn

into

into the Snare, "Child, write down this Reprimand, that you may remember it all your Life, to hinder you from ever setting a Step out of the sure Road of holy Obedience." So great a Love she had for the State of a simple Religious, that she was often heard to say, that she wished she could have put it in her Vows, never to have borne any Office. She was very careful that no worldly Customs should be introduced into the Monastery; saying, they are the Poison of a religious State; for as soon as the Spirit of the World finds any Admittance into a Convent, the Spirit of God forsakes it. Her great Desire of living sequestered, and unknown to the World, made her decline, as much as possible, all secular Conversation at the Speak-house, never going thither, except on urgent Occasions, when her Presence was absolutely requisite, and then with great Reluctance: for it was her only Delight to live in Solitude with her amiable Jesus, She would often repeat to her Sisters: O blessed Solitude! sole Beatitude!

Her holy Zeal and Devotion. Retirement was her Paradise, or we may rather say, that in it God made her Soul an interiour Pa-

Paradise, in which she always enjoyed his divine Presence, by the Exercises of the most tender and sweet Devotion. For though she excelled in every Virtue more than can be expressed, or even be imagined by those who have not had the Happiness of having been thoroughly acquainted with her, nothing was so admirable as her eminent and sublime Spirit of Prayer. She had the highest Esteem for publick Prayer, and made it her first Care to endeavour that the Manner in which the divine Office was constantly performed in her Monastery, might be as much as possible, an Imitation of the heavenly Choir of Angels, and all the blessed Spirits, singing the divine Praises before the Throne of God, in the Sanctuary of his Glory. In a short Book which she wrote for the Use and Direction of her spiritual Children and put into their Hands, under this Title: *Prayers and Considerations upon each Article of the holy Rule of the Poor Clares.* Upon the third Article she inculcates in the strongest and most pathetick Manner possible, the Diligence and Respect with which every one is to assist at the divine Office, without ever failing, in the least Circumstance,

stance, and adds the following Reflection:
"This is the principal Service of God,
"there being nothing on Earth which
"represents more perfectly the State of
"the Blessed in Heaven, than to praise
"him with Fervour and Cheerfulness.
"For it is written: *Happy are they who
"dwell in the House of God, to bless and
"praise him eternally.* It is the perpe-
"tual Employment of the Angels and
"religious Persons, being Angels on
"Earth, ought as much as possible, to
"imitate the Angels of Heaven. O my
"Soul, praise thy Lord and thy God,
"to whom belong all Praise and Glory,
"in Heaven and on Earth. O God of
"Glory and Majesty, from thy Throne
"proceedeth a Voice, which says to all
"the Inhabitants of the celestial *Jerusa-
"lem:* Give Praise and Benediction to
"God, all you that are here. O that
"every Moment of my Life I might
"praise thee, bless thee, give thee
"Thanks for thy great Glory. O most
"great, most glorious, most bountiful
"Lord God, I adore thee from the Cen-
"tre of my Nothing. Give me Grace,
"that I may always offer to thee the Sa-
"crifice of Praise with Fervour of Spirit,
"that

"that so it may be acceptable to thee.
"Stay, I beseech thee, the Powers of
"my Soul, especially my wandring Ima-
"gination, that in the Beginning, Con-
"tinuance, and End of this Angelical
"Exercise, I always keep myself in thy
"divine Presence." In another Place she writes: "O my God, I wish I had all the
"Awe and Respect with which the An-
"gels and twenty-four Elders are pene-
"trated, when they prostrate themselves
"before the Lamb. Strike me with an
"holy Fear, and let me be plunged in
"Adoration of the Greatness of thy so-
"vereign Majesty, and penetrated with
"a Sense of my own Baseness, to the
"End, that if I cannot, like them, offer
"thee, a pure Heart, all burning with
"Love, I may at least offer thee an hum-
"ble Heart, and assist in thy Presence
"with as great Reverence, Attention,
"Devotion, and Humility, as I am able.
"When will it be, O sovereign Majesty,
"that I shall praise thee like the Angels?
"When shall I love thee perfectly?
"Happy are they who praise thee eter-
"nally. Make me of this Number by
"thine infinite Mercy. O blessed St. *Collet*,
"who like a celestial Nightingale, spent
"all

"all thy Strength in singing the Praises of thy Creator, whilst here below, and art now keeping a Concert with the Choirs of Angels in the celestial *Jerusalem*, pray for me, that I may so Love and praise God in this Life, that I may one Day enter into the Temple of Glory, to praise and bless him eternally in thy happy Company. Amen." In a little Directory of the Nuns, for the regulating well all their Actions, according to the Spirit of their Rule, which she compiled for them under this Title: *The Chief Points of our holy Ceremonies, in which the Sisters must daily renew themselves in Spirit, and in their Actions;* she begins with laying down Rules for the divine Office, as follows. Point 1. "The Sisters must be diligent and ready in going to the Choir at the first Sound of the Bell, leaving imperfect the Work they are about, rather than staying to finish it. The holy Scripture speaking of the most pure and elevated among the celestial Spirits, maketh an Abridgment of all their Greatness and Privileges, by saying, that they assist always before the Throne of God. Nothing can be greater than such an "Ho-

" Honour. The Sisters must therefore
" repair diligently, and with great Joy
" into this Sanctuary, there to adore the
" Holy of Holies. What a Consolation
" for a Soul full of Faith and Love, to
" be always present before our Lord, to
" prostrate herself at the Feet of Jesus
" Christ, to pour out her Heart in his
" Presence, whilst the whole World is
" overwhelmed with Affliction and Mi-
" sery." 2d. Point. " They must keep
" their Sight under a strict Guard in all
" Places, but particularly in the Choir,
" and at all Prayer. It is an excellent
" Means to keep their Thoughts and
" Hearts recollected, and to cut off an
" Infinity of Distractions. Happy that
" Soul which closes her Eyes to exteriour
" and perishable Things, that she may
" never, if possible, lose Sight of her
" sovereign and only true Good." 3d.
Point. " They must stand upright and
" handsomely in the Choir, remember-
" ing that Jesus Christ beholds them,
" also his holy Angels. Let them con-
" sider how these blessed Spirits abase
" themselves with Reverence and Respect
" before the infinite Majesty of God;
" how they tremble in his Presence. And
                                    " shall

"shall poor Dust and Ashes dare to stand
"in an irreligious Posture before her
"Lord and Master? The infinite Mer-
"cies of Jesus Christ, and his astonish-
"ing Humiliation in the holy Eucharist,
"far from diminishing, ought to increase
"our Respect. The more his Love
"makes him forget what he is, the more
"ought we to bear in Mind what we are,
"and what he is." 4th. Point. "They
"must keep strict Silence in the Church,
"and this as well with their Bodies and
"Limbs, as with their Tongues. This
"has always been esteemed a Thing so
"sacred that, as the Scripture tells us,
"when the Temple of *Solomon* was built,
"God commanded that there should not
"be heard so much as the Sound of an
"Hammer, or any other Instrument.
"Every one must therefore carefully
"avoid making any Noise, both out of
"Respect to the Presence of Jesus Christ;
"and also not to give the least Occasion
"of Distraction to their Sisters." 5th.
Point. "They must go out of the
"Church with great Gravity and Mo-
"desty. For a religious Person, that
"comes from conversing with God, ought
"to appear rather as an Angel, than as

"an

" an Angel, than as an human Creature,
" all penetrated with his divine Presence,
" Sanctity and Modesty ought to shine
" in their Exteriour. These Virtues will
" render them accessible to all, respected
" by all, &c." Our venerable Abbess was the most perfect Model of these Rules, and of perfect Devotion, at the divine Office. She never spared Voice or Strength to have it upheld, and performed in the best Manner. On all Solemnities she began and gave it out with such Devotion, as if her Heart was really in Heaven, and enjoyed the happy Vision of God. During all the Time, by her lively Faith, and the Ardour of her Love and Zeal, she seemed, as it were, quite absorpt in God, and her Countenance appeared so Angelical, that to cast an Eye upon her was enough to inspire the most Tepid with Fervour. It was seldom but her Cheeks were all bathed in Tears. Yet notwithstanding her profound Recollection, such was her Vigilance over the Choir, that no Faults escaped her, which could be committed by any one in reading, or in the least Circumstance of their Behaviour, which she never failed to correct by a speedy Reprehension and publick

lick Penance, in order to make a Reparation.

The sacred Passion of our divine Redeemer, and the adorable Sacrament of the Altar, were two infinitely tender Objects of her Devotion, in which she found her sweetest Delight and Comfort. The moving and lively Manner in which she expressed herself on them, discovered the burning Sentiments of her Heart, and her sublime enlightened Ideas of of these great Mysteries. By many little Prayers to honour them, which she compiled, and gave to her spiritual Children, she studied to stir up in them the same Sentiments of Devotion. Her lively Faith and Love made her think all Time short, which she employed herself in the like Exercises. For she spent whole Hours, or rather her whole Time, when other Duties did not call her away, in holy Meditation and Prayer, in which the Life and Sufferings of Christ, and the holy Mystery of the Eucharist made usually a principal Part. On solemn Festivals, and whenever the blessed Eucharist was exposed, she remained very long in the Church, with her Eyes and Heart fixed on that adorable Sacrament, as if she

she had been immoveable. Under her most painful Distempers, when she could not assist at Matins with the Sisters, after they were retired to Rest, she spent every Night, at least, one Hour in Prayer before the holy Sacrament. In a Course of short Exercises, for the pious Visits of our Redeemer, in this tremendous Mystery, she considers Him in his different Qualities and Attributes on different Days. 1st. As the Son of God, adored by the Angels and Saints in Heaven, with whom she desired to join her Voice, and sing: *Holy, Holy, Holy, the Heavens and the Earth are filled with the Majesty of thy Glory.* 2dly. As a consuming Fire, begging Him in profound Love and Adoration to consume in her all terrestrial Affections, and whatever could put an Impediment to her perfect Union with Him, which He desired in this Sacrament. 3dly. As an inaccessible shining Light, though covered with a Veil toward the Earth, to accommodate Himself to our weak Sight, which cannot bear its immense Effulgence: And she begs that the Brightness of this Sun may enlighten all that is dark in her Soul. 4thly. As the Author of Grace and Sanctity, which she desires to approach, begging to partake of His Fullness, and drink of the Torrent of Delights which He communicates to Souls, which for His Love contemn all earthly Things. 5thly. As the Gift of God, including all other Gifts, equal to, and really Himself; and she begs the Grace to praise and thank Him for all his Mercies and Benefits. 6thly. As the Abridgment of all the Works of God; the Sacrament which gives Grace and Sanctity to the Just, and Strength to Sinners, excites Admiration in the Angels, and gives Joy to the Saints in Heaven; and she begs to be enabled to frame a true Idea of his Greatness, and to be firmly united to Him by the Band of Love. 7thly. As the Mystery of Love, and she admires how infinitely He deserves all our Love, and begs to correspond to the utmost of her Abilities. 8thly. As our Head, and begs that He govern all that is in her. 9thly. As our Physician, and begs to be healed by Him. 10thly, as our Centre, and begs her Heart, which can find no Satisfaction out of Him, may rest in Him alone. 11thly. As our only Lover, crying out, *Give me thy Heart*; and she presents

sents to Him her Heart, all defiled, as it is, with disordered Affections, and says to him a Million of Times: "Pierce my "Heart with the Dart of thy Love.--- "O my God, be the Comfort of my "Banishment, allay my Grief; for to "Thee sighs every Desire of my Heart, "&c."

This devout Lover of Jesus was commonly observed by the Sisters to prepare herself for the holy Communion with Floods of Tears of most sweet Devotion. With regard to that holy Sacrament, it was not easy to discern which made the stronger Impression upon her Soul; a profound Humility which convinced her of her great Unworthiness, or her ardent Love, which made her sigh continually after that Bread of Life, in which she found, as she often said, all her Comfort and Support, and her main Resource under all the Miseries, Dangers, and Trials of this Life. In her last Sickness, when she was confined to her Bed, she seemed to redouble her continual earnest Sighs, and pious Breathings after this heavenly Food, and she had it brought to her, and received it with her usual lively Faith and Love, once a Week, very

very early in the Morning, becaufe fhe could not remain Fafting. The Day after her Heart ufed to be fo inflamed with divine Love, that when the Phyfician came to fee her, her Words filled him with Devotion, infomuch that he could fcarce refolve to leave her. After Communion fhe was wholly penetrated with the Goodnefs and Mercy of our Redeemer, fo as to feem to forget all Things of this World. Being once afked how fhe employed thofe precious Moments, fhe feemed to think that it was not eafy to exprefs it, but replied, " My dear Child, " I make ufe of thefe Words: O Soul of " Jefus Chrift fanctify me: Blood of Je- " fus Chrift cleanfe me: Body of Jefus " Chrift fave me, &c." It is not eafily imagined how fenfibly fhe was affected when fhe faw any one abfent herfelf from that life-giving Food, and fhe could not be fatisfied till fhe fent for the Perfon to know the Reafon, and to endeavour to be a Help and Comfort to her, and to excite her Fervour, or take Care that her Difficulties were fpeedily removed. At the Holy Mafs fhe feemed always to affift in Extafy of Devotion. She partly compofed, and partly extracted from the

the Works of the pious F. *Simon Gourdan*, and others, moſt pathetick ſhort Conſiderations and Devotions on all the Actions and Circumſtances of the ſacred Life and Sufferings of our divine Saviour, recorded in the Goſpels, adding Acts of Adoration, Praiſe, and Love for each, begging his Grace by each, and ſtudying in every one of them to enter into, and learn His perfect Spirit of Virtue, in order to form her Heart upon the Model of His divine Heart. She compiled like Devotions on the chief Attributes of the Divinity, and each of the three divine Perſons, and on all the great Myſteries of our Religion, which are honoured in the principal Feſtivals of the Year. She diverſified theſe Devotions in ſuch a lively Manner, and prepared herſelf with ſuch admirable Fervour, and ſuch particular Sentiments of Piety, for every Solemnity in the Year, that one might juſtly have thought each to have been her principal Feſtival of Devotion. Indeed one who is accuſtomed in a Spirit of Prayer, to live in a conſtant amorous Application of her Powers to the Preſence of God, who fills and employs her Heart and Underſtanding, ſo contemplates God in each Myſtery, as to be animated by it, and filled with its Spirit, in a more perfect Manner, by a short, even inftantaneous Contemplation, than another would be by long Reflections.

Her Devotion to the holy Mother of God was moft remarkable; with fingular Veneration and Confidence fhe ftyled her with the Church, the Refuge of poor Sinners, and the Comfort of the Afflicted. In all Difficulties fhe had recourfe to her, and ftrongly recommended the fame to all under her Care. She thought fhe fhould have failed in a principal Part of her Duty, had fhe not joined to this glorious Virgin her bleffed Spoufe St. *Jofeph*, whom fhe often called her Father and Protector, and the Patron of her Community. She put herfelf and them, in a particular Manner, under his Protection, both in Regard to fpirituals and temporals; before his Feftival it was her earneft Endeavour to excite and renew their Devotion to this great Saint, and their Confidence in his Patronage. For in all Neceffities, amongft all the heavenly Interceffors, next to the holy Mother of God, fhe had recourfe to St. *Jofeph*, and frequently found the Effects of his powerful Interceffion, by very remarkable

Blef-

Blessings. She had likewise a great Devotion to St. *Michael*, the Guardian Angels, and all the Choirs of heavenly Spirits, and compiled several beautiful Exercises in their Honour, especially on their seraphick Love of God, and Ardour in praising and glorifying his holy Name. One of these Exercises she closes with the following Prayer. " Obtain for me, ar-
" dent Seraphims, some Sparks of your
" Flames: Blessed Cherubims, some Ir-
" radiations of your Light: holy Thrones,
" a Participation of your Peace: excel-
" lent Dominations, a couragious Empire
" over all my Passions: Sacred Virtues, a
" Share of your Strength against the
" Enemies of Jesus Christ, awful Pow-
" ers, your Authority over Devils, glo-
" rious Principalities, your Zeal for the
" Honour of the most High God: holy
" Archangels, your Ardour for the De-
" fence and Propagation of the Church,
" and the Sanctity of its Mysteries:
" blessed Angels, your charitable Care
" for the Salvation of Men: and you
" seven Princes, who stand always be-
" fore the Throne of God, and the Lamb,
" make me break with you the same
" Bread of Heaven, in the Contempla-
" tion

"tion of the same God, and may I be
"like you, all inflamed, and entirely
"transformed into Love. O invincible
"Defenders of the Reign of Jesus Christ,
"all penetrated with Zeal for his Glory,
"and for the Establishment of his Wor-
"ship, let me breathe nothing but his
"Mysteries, his Maxims, his Virtues,
"and his divine Spirit. May I subject to
"Him all my Powers, and the very Cen-
"tre of my Heart, that having glorified
"Him on Earth with an Homage of Ado-
"ration and Obedience like yours, I may
"contemplate Him one Day in the Splen-
"dours of a blessed Immortality, and
"present Him with you eternal Canticles
"of Praise and Love. Amen."

This her Devotion to the blessed Angels and Saints, sprang from the Ardour of her Love of God, whom these holy Spirits love with all their Strength, and praise without Interruption. To entertain and improve this Love of God, which, as she observes, is the only Scope, Aim, and End of all our Exercises, Labours, Austerities, and Works of Piety, she drew up many Forms of the most inflamed Acts of that Virtue, by which she ceased not most earnestly to ask it of God

God. "O my most sweet Lord Jesus," says she, in her MS. Considerations on the Rule, ch. 6. "Give me this Love. Draw to "thyself all the Powers of my Soul. I "ask of thee, O Lord, no earthly Trea- "sures, no worldly Goods or Glory. I "beg only the Riches of Thy pure Love, "that in all Things I may seek Thee "alone, prize thee above all, be con- "tent with Thee alone, who art to me "All in All. O Love of my God, the "Life of my Soul, the Crown of my "Head, the Centre of all my Affecti- "ons. To Thee I consecrate all my Ac- "tions; to Thee I dedicate irrevocably "all my Labours and Desires; all I am "or have; I will not live, my God, but "to love Thee; I will not breathe, but "to glorify Thee. O that I could break "forth without Intermission, into sera- "phick Acts of Thy Love, O my most "amiable Lord! O that I could conti- "nue to repeat them each Moment of "my Life! Particularly, may I die in the "highest Raptures of this Love." Other such ardent Breathings occur, ch. 5. ib. and in many other Parts of her Writings.

In the same she intersperses frequent warm Aspirations and Sighs to be dissolv-
ed,

ed and united with her God, and his Chrift in eternal Glory, that fhe may love and praife Him without Intermiffion, with all her Powers and Strength. For this fhe compiled *Brief Rules for the Pilgrims who tend to the celeftial Jerufalem.* The firft fhe lays down as follows: "They "muft endeavour to be Deaf, Dumb, "and Blind to all Things that do not "concern them. They muft love Si- "lence, Recollection and Prayer, and "practice thefe as much as their State "and Employments permit." After other Rules for the Direction of the Pilgrim Soul through the Defert of this World, by perfect Charity, Meeknefs, and Patience; entire Difengagement of the Heart, Mortification of the Senfes, Spirit of Compunction and Penance, Love of Poverty and the Crofs, Humility, and the utmoft Fidelity in directing every Action to fulfill the holy Will of God with the greateft Fervour, and purity of Intention poffible, fhe is taught to figh without Intermiffion after the happy Hour which will finifh her Exile. A long Exercife is fubjoined, confifting of pathetick Confiderations and Afpirations for every Day, during a Courfe of fix Months,

Months, then to be begun again. They all express the languishing Desires of a Pilgrim Soul to be united to her God, and are chiefly extracted from the Book entitled, *Le Chretien etranger sur la terre*, but very much abridged, improved, and presented in a more pathetick Manner, and much clearer Order. By those laid down for the first Month, the Pilgrim Soul is prepared by Compunction and Penance, to attain to Innocence and Cleanness of Heart; by holy Fear to loosen and break all earthly Attachments, to extinguish in her Heart all Desire of pleasing Creatures; to watch continually over herself against Vanity and Pride; to raise herself above all human Respects; to have before her Eyes, in all that she does, only God and his Glory; to be affected, as if there were only God and herself in the World, and by all Manner of good Works, and the Exercise of all Virtues, to have her Lamp always trimmed in her Hands, ready to go forth to meet her Bridegroom, and sighing continually after him. The Exercises for the second Month are employed on Death, as the Passage of a Soul to her God. In those for the third the World is

consi-

considered as an Exile. The fourth is taken up in Contemplations on the Bliss of Heaven, and in languishing Sighs after God. The two last Months are consecrated to Exercises which tend to inspire an ardent Love of God, and Fervour in the Practice of His holy Law, the Means by which the Pilgrim Soul advances in the Path of spotless Sanctity and Love, to a perfect Possession of God, who is infinite tremendous Sanctity, and infinite Love.

The Zeal of the holy Abbess for the spiritual Progress of her whole Community, prompted her to prescribe to every one little Practices of Devotion, suitable to each one's spiritual Necessities and Dispositions, which, notwithstanding her Infirmities, she used to write with her own Hand: As, to live on Earth, as in a wild vast Desert, continually sighing toward Heaven; or to live, as if there were only God and them, in constant Attention to Him, &c. She was ever proposing to them various easy Means and Methods to help them to practise a continual Attention to the divine Presence. For this End she also wrote short fervent Ejaculations for every Place and Em-

Employment. Before *Lent* and *Advent* she drew up in Writing, for every young Nun, certain Instructions, according as she judged most suitable to every one's particular Circumstances and Necessities, and these she put in the Cell of each one, written with her own Hand. To this her Zeal, Prudence, and unwearied Charity, is her Monastery indebted for an incredible Number of short excellent MS. Instructions, Prayers, and several longer Treatises, as 1. *An Exercise of Devotion on the Life of Christ for every Day of the Year.* 2. *Exercises for the principal Festivals.* 3. *Exercises on the holy Angels.* 4. *Brief Rules for the Pilgrims who tend to the celestial Jerusalem, with Exercises for every Day, during a Course of six Months.* 5. *A Collection of little Offices and Litanies on the several Mysteries of the Life of our Saviour: Also on the Virgin Mary and St. Joseph.* 6. *Entertainment on Christ's glorious Life,* or on the State of his glorious Immortality. 7. *A Book of Devotions to Jesus, on the Mystery of His Incarnation,* and others to the Blessed Virgin and St. Joseph. 8. *Litanies and other Devotions to the holy Solitaries, especially St. John the Silent.* 9. *Devotions to St. Mary Magdalen,*

dalen, St. Mary of Egypt, St. Thais, and other holy *Penitents,* especially *Solitaries.* 10. Exercises for hearing *Mass,* &c. 11. Prayers and Considerations upon each Article of the Rule of the Poor Clares, in which the Spirit in which every Duty ought to be performed, is excellently inculcated, especially on Obedience, Silence and Devotion. On this last she strongly exhorts the Sisters to be careful never to extinguish in their Souls the Spirit of Prayer and Devotion, by suffering their Thoughts to be so much taken up with, or bent upon their Work, or their corporal Strength so exhausted with it, or so much of their Time taken up by it, as to make them neglect, or become unfit for Prayer, holy Meditation, or other Exercises of Piety. Whence she takes Occasion to enlarge on the Excellencies of *Incomparable Devotion,* which is derived to us from the Father of Lights, to draw Men up from Earth to Heaven. She calls it the Art to make our Souls divine; the sweet and sacred Entertainment of all who desire to love God, and the dear and only Darling of our Souls. 12. She wrote, as was mentioned above, a little Directory for her Community, entitled,

The

The Chief Points of our holy Ceremonies, in which the Sisters must daily renew themselves in Spirit, and in their Actions. In this little Treatise she gives excellent Instructions, particularly on Prayer, Obedience, and Silence, by which we cut off the Source of many Sins, build in our Hearts a Temple for the Holy Ghost, and practise a Virtue which easily produces, cultivates, and preserves all other Virtues. On fraternal Charity she writes, ch. 7. " We must have a tender cor-
" dial Love for all, accompanied with
" Respect, preventing each other in every
" Service, shunning all Disputes, as the
" Seed of Dissention, always ready to
" leave our own Will and Judgment to
" conform to others, to bear each other's
" Burdens, support each other's Ways
" and Humours, never complaining of
" any one's Behaviour, and behaving
" toward all with Sweetness, by which
" we may change Antipathy into Love."
On Poverty she says, ch. 9, " To disen-
" gage our Hearts from the Love of all
" transitory Things, we must take for
" ourselves the worst and meanest Part
" in every Thing, and desire nothing of
" this World, that we may fix our Af-
" fections

"fections where our Treasure ought to
"be." On Humility, ch. 10. "To be
"poor and proud is abominable before
"God and Men. We muſt therefore
"have a mean Opinion of ourſelves in
"all Things, be ready ſincerely to take
"upon ourſelves any Fault, of which
"we are accuſed, to acknowledge it,
"and make Satisfaction; bow to each
"other, when we paſs by, eſteeming
"ourſelves happy to ſerve any one, and
"unworthy to be ſerved by any one;
"bear a great Reſpect and Love to all,
"as to the Spouſes of Jeſus Chriſt."
After other Rules ſhe concludes with
theſe Words: "Dear Siſters, I leave
"you this as my laſt Will and Teſta-
"ment, and as a Token of the ſincere
"Love and Tenderneſs I have for you,
"deſiring above all Things, your ſpiri-
"tual Advancement. I therefore beg
"you read theſe Inſtructions once a
"Month, and endeavour to practiſe
"them, which will draw the Bleſſing of
"God upon you in this Life, and an
"eternal Reward in the next. Pray for
"me, your unworthy Mother and Ser-
"vant, Siſter *Mary* of the Holy Croſs.
"the 8th of *September*, 1726.

This

This holy Contemplative was indeed endowed with an excellent Understanding and Judgment, and at the same Time grounded in the most sincere and profound Humility, so as always to esteem herself as the least and last Person in the House: all she did she reputed as Nothing, and bore the sharpest Trials with invincible Meekness and Patience, saying, her Sins deserved much more. In a lively Sense of the Judgments of God, and of the heavy Weight of her Charge, she sighed to the End of her life after the Happiness of living a private Nun, if it could have been allowed. Her most humble Opinion, and perfect Contempt of herself appeared most conspicuous amidst the extraordinary Respect and Esteem, which her Virtue procured her from all who had the Happiness of her Acquaintance, especially of her religious Sisters, of whom she herself received thirty-four to Profession, during the Time she was Abbess. Indeed she was the best of Mothers to all her dear Children, continually going before them, as a bright shining Torch, teaching and exhorting them by Word and Example, what they were to do to please their heavenly Spouse, and to keep

up

up in every Point of their holy Rule to the moſt exact Regularity. It was her whole Study to bring them on to Perfection, and to maintain Piety, Peace, and perfect Union amongſt them. The following Inſtructions to her Succeſſors were found after her Death, in her own Handwriting: " I beg of thoſe that hold this
" Place after me, that they take great
" Care whom they receive, and that
" they never admit any who cannot be
" told of a Fault, or who cannot conform
" in all Things to the Ways, Practices,
" Cuſtoms, and Ceremonies of this holy
" Religious State, nor give any the little
" Habit of Poſtulants before they are
" ſixteen complete, nor the great Habit
" (or Habit of the Order) till after a
" Trial of ſix Months. The long Experience I have had, makes me ſee
" the Neceſſity of theſe Precautions.---
" Never admit any to religious Vows,
" who cannot leave their own Will,
" even in good Things.---Never admit
" any who ſhew a Diſlike of their Miſ-
" treſs: for infallibly they will afterward
" take one to their Superiour.---Never
" receive any who come too late to all
" Duties: they will ſoon be diſguſted
" with

" with their Vocation, and come at last
" to nothing, at least by their good
" Will.---Never take any who are of a
" gibing Temper, for they will never
" keep Charity with their Sisters, but
" will be always raising Brawls and
" Quarrels.---Be very strict upon them
" in observing Silence, in keeping their
" Sight under constant Guard, and in
" walking in a religious Pace, with their
" Hands joined, and their Hearts lifted
" up to Heaven.---Never suffer them to
" take Notice of any one's Actions or
" Comportment, be they never so pub-
" lick; nor meddle with the Affairs of
" the House: Those that are given to
" these Faults, are not fit for a religious
" State.---Those who cannot leave them-
" selves in good Things, will at last be
" obstinate in bad Things, and will be-
" come incorrigible.---Those that con-
" temn little Things, will soon contemn
" greater.---Those who take a Dislike to
" their Mistress, shew an ungrateful Spi-
" rit, and will never make any Progress
" in Virtue.---Those who come always
" late, will soon lose their first Fervour,
" and the Spirit of Religion, which is
" maintained by a constant Perseverance
" in

"in doing our Duty readily, and with
"Fervour.---Those who are given to ly-
"ing and bantering will soon be the
"Destroyers of Peace and Union in a
"Community, as well as endanger their
"own Souls.---Never admit any who
"shew but little Esteem of small Things,
"though it should be only a little Cere-
"mony.---I most humbly confess and
"acknowledge I have never done my
"own Duty, and shall, by my own Neg-
"ligence and bad Conduct, leave the
"Community in a much worse State
"than I found it, which I attribute to
"my own Presumption, and a secret
"Confidence I had in myself. Hoping
"to have reformed lesser Abuses, I have
"contracted far greater Faults. God of
"his infinite Mercy pardon me, and
"grant that those who come after me may
"have better Success. Amen. Amen."
This Confession her Humility and holy
Fear extorted from her; but it is noto-
rious to all who knew the Monastery
that she left it much improved, especially in Spirituals. It is remarkable,
that in the Devotions, Instructions, and
whole Conduct of this holy Contemplative, every Thing was perfectly solid,

prudent,

prudent, and exact, entirely free from all Circumstances which could be charged with Weakness, and particularly from any of the false Principles of the *Demi-Quietists*, or other false Mysticks, which had found Abettors of great Reputation in *Normandy*, and some of them had caused no small Confusion and Disturbance in this Monastery, before she was chosen Abbess, but were easily banished by her superiour Discretion, Piety, Knowledge, and Experience.

It pleased God to visit the holy Abbess with painful Distempers for the last ten Years of her Life, that nothing might be wanting to complete her Sacrifice, and that being tried in the Furnace, and prepared by the Exercise of all heroick Virtues, she might be raised to the sublime Glory of the Saints. She suffered racking Pains a long Time from cruel Fits of the Stone, and after this an Ulcer in her Kidneys, which soon brought her to such a Degree of Weakness, that from that Time to her Death, she could never walk without the Help of another, nor ever kneel down only for a Moment, when she received the holy Communion. Nevertheless, she never failed till the last Year,

Year, to come to all the Hours of the divine Office of the Day, and on great Days to Matins at Midnight, and in Summer also to the Refectory, suffering with incredible Sweetness and Patience all the Inconveniences of her Distempers. She was never wanting in any Branch of her Duties, in governing her Monastery, or in attending to the particular Necessities, and spiritual Good of every one of the Sisters, as if she had enjoyed her Strength and perfect Health, till the last seven Months of her Life, when her Disorders had brought on a most painful Dropsy, which swelled her whole Body. She continued always to bear her Pains with such Calmness, Cheerfulness, and Silence, that to see her one would have thought she suffered nothing at all; and her accustomed Sweetness and Serenity never left her to the last Moment of her Life. Her Soul seemed continually united to God,

Her Death.

by devout Prayer, and she earnestly sighed after Heaven. When the Physician said one Day, that she was not yet near her End, she said to a Sister that was near her: "Alas! Child, my "Pilgrimage is prolonged. When the last

last Sacraments were ordered, she washed her own Hands with great Cheerfulness and Tranquility, and called for clean Linen, out of Zeal to observe, to the last Moment of her Life, the least Ceremony of the Rule. Then she said, "Now the Hour is come that there is no Comfort but in Jesus Christ. Talk not to me of this or that Devotion. Jesus Christ is my whole Support. All Good is due only to his Grace. I am a poor weak Creature." She had received the holy Viaticum on the 17th of *March*, and Extreme Unction the next Day. She would needs speak to every Sister in particular, though she was then reduced to the last Degree of Weakness, and they were above fifty in Number. She asked Pardon of every one for any Fault she might have committed in their Regard, or any Pain or Uneasiness she might have ever given them; and afterward gave each some good Advice, according to their particular Necessities, which they received with Hearts ready to burst with Grief, seeing themselves upon the Point of losing so incomparable and so holy a Superior and spiritual Mother. She particularly exhorted them to Peace and Union in the Election of a Superiour, and to live always in a holy Submission to Heaven, content whatever fell out. After this she desired the History of our Lord's Passion to be often read to her, on which, from her habitual Devotion to those adorable Mysteries, she entertained herself with the most perfect Sentiments of Love, Adoration, Thanksgiving, Praise, Compunction, Humility, Resignation, Oblation, Supplication, fraternal Charity, and all other Virtues. The next Day she lost her Speech, but survived yet three Days, during which she seemed to suffer very much, though always with the same constant Peace, Tranquility, heavenly Devotion, and holy Joy in her Countenance. On the third Day, about half an Hour after Eight, she sweetly yielded up her pious Soul to her Creator, on the 21st of *March*, in the Year 1735, the 82d of her Age, the 60th of her religious Profession, and the 23d of her Government of the Monastery, in the Office of Abbess. May God, in his gracious Mercy, bestow on us a Share in her eminent Spirit of his holy Love, of Humility, Compunction and

Prayer,

Prayer, that we may courageously walk in the Steps of his faithful Servants, and happily arrive at the Kingdom of his Glory. Amen. Amen.

CONCLUSION.

FROM the Example of the Servants of God we learn the true Meaning of those important Words of our dear Redeemer: *Behold, the Kingdom of God is within you* (21). If we are unacquainted with the Happiness of this Grace, if we are not possessed of this inestimable Treasure, the Fault lies in us. He will not, he cannot establish in our Hearts the Reign of his Grace and holy Love, so long as we refuse to dispose and prepare our Souls to receive his sweet Law, and perhaps entertain Dispositions diametrically opposite. To belong to God, much more to invite him to reign in us, we must first banish his Enemy, destroy his Empire in us, renounce all Intelligence with him, and cast away all his Arms and Instruments, by cutting off all Occasions of Sin, and flying its Snares

(21) *Luke*, xvii. 21.

Snares and Dangers. It is farther neceſſary to die to the World and our Senſes, to cut off all inordinate Attachments to earthly Things, and to have crucified the Old Man in us, that by a perfect Purity of Heart, all Obſtacles to the Reign of the divine Spirit in our Affections may be removed. This is not a light Work, but requires the moſt ſerious Application. Nor muſt we ſtop here. The fervent Practice of all Virtues is likewiſe neceſſary. Prayer itſelf, without this Support from the active Life, is too Weak for ſo great a Work. Hence it appears why many have ſpent ſeveral Years in the aſſiduous Exerciſes of holy Meditation and Prayer, without making any Progreſs in a ſpiritual Life. The Reaſon is, they are wedded to their own Humour, ſtill foſter in their Breaſts many favourite petty Paſſions, and do not ſtrenuouſly labour to kill the Seeds which ſhoot out many poiſonous Suckers, by which the whole Circle of their Lives, even their Virtues themſelves, are often tainted.

When the Soil of the Heart is prepared, (which Preparation itſelf is carried on chiefly by the Aſſiſtance of humble Prayer) this

this holy Exercise is made the omnipotent Instrument of divine Grace, in the wonderful inward Reformation of the Soul. Prayer purifies the Mind, the Fountain from whence it springs, says S. *John Climacus*: it drives away Darkness, and replenishes the Understanding with heavenly Light; it heals the Disorders of the Will, purges the Affections from inordinate earthly Attachments, raises them to heavenly Things, and makes the Soul spiritual, and akin to the Angels, nay, by uniting the Soul with God, makes it, in some Measure, divine. Therefore a Life of Prayer is the great Means of raising the Soul to perfect Virtue, and is the very Soul of a religious State. Hence Abbot *Isaac*, a most experienced Director among the ancient Monks of *Scete*, defined the End of the Monastick State, and the Summit of Christian Perfection, to be the most perfect Spirit of Prayer (22). And again (23):
 "This is the End which every Monk
 "must propose to himself, this ought
 "to be his whole Aim, that he may pos-
 "sess in this Body an Image of the Fe-

" licity to come, and begin to receive
" in this World a certain Pledge of that
" heavenly Conversation and Glory. This
" I say is the End of all Perfection,
" that the Mind, purged from all car-
" nal Attachment, may be daily raised
" to spiritual Things, till its whole Con-
" versation, and every Motion of the
" Heart may be made one uninterrupted
" Prayer." The same great Master of a
spiritual Life, lays down the Rules by
which the Spirit of Prayer, the Summit
of Christian Perfection, and the great
Art of divine Love, may be most se-
curely and most readily attained. He
says that, in order to become Men of
Prayer, we must, 1st. when we pray, retire with Christ to the Mountain, at least,
shut our Eyes, all our Senses, and all the
Faculties of our Soul, to all earthly Objects, and whatever is not God (24).
2dly. We must study to live at all Times
disentangled from earthly Attachments
and Passions, and habitually recollected,
as Prudence, and the Circumstances of
every one's State will allow; for such
will every one be found in Prayer, as he
usually is at other Times (25); which
Maxim

(24) Coll. 10. c. 6.   (25) Ib. c. 14.

Maxim is strongly inculcated by S. *John Climacus.* 3dly. We must much accustom ourselves to frequent Prayer, holy Meditation, and Watchings, or Prayer in the Silence of the Night(26). 4thly. The assiduous Practice of continual Prayer, by frequent fervent Aspirations in all our ordinary Actions, will much facilitate this Exercise. This holy Abbot recommends the habitual Use of some particular Aspiration, by which a Person will always have it at Hand. For this he much commends that Versicle of the Psalm, *Deus in adjutorium meum intende. Domine, ad adjuvandum me festina* (27). Of which he says: " This Versicle appo-
" sitely admits all Sentiments of Piety,
" which the human Heart can form, and
" is a Weapon adapted to repel every
" Assault of the Enemy. For it ex-
" presses an Invocation of God, the
" Humility of a pious Confession, the
" Solicitude of perpetual Watchfulness
" and Fear, the Consideration of our
" own Frailty, (which is the very Ab-
" stract of Weakness and Misery) a
" Confidence of being heard through
God's

(26) Ib. and S. *Greg.* m. l. 26. Moral. c. 36, 37, &c.   (27) Ps. lxix.

"God's mercy; an Assurance that He is
"our Protector, and always present. It
"contains, in our Recourse to God, a
"fervent Aspiration of divine Love, and
"a constant Watchfulness and Fear of
"the Snares of the Enemy, and our
"continual Dangers; in all their As-
"saults it is an impregnable Rampart,
"an impenetrable Helmet, and a Shield
"which foils every Dart. It raises the
"Courage of those that are depressed,
"gives Comfort to the Afflicted, and
"humbles those that are elate with Pros-
"perity, or tempted with Pride. It
"gives Strength and Resolution under
"every Temptation, and secures Victory
"over every Enemy. If the Spirit of
"Gluttony prompts to break the Fast
"before the Hour; if you are tempted
"to Vain-glory, &c. cry out with Ear-
"nestness, Love, and Humility: *Deus*
"*in adjutorium, &c.* Let your Meditation
"on this Verse always fill your Breast
"Night and Day, at Home and Abroad,
"in Prosperity and Adversity; repeat it
"in every Action and every Necessity:
"have it in your Mouth when Sleep
"steals upon you, and so assiduously,
"that by Habit you may repeat it, per-
                                     "chance,

" chance, even in your Sleep. When
" you awake let this anticipate all other
" Thoughts, and fill first your Heart,
" and form your first Words: In rising
" let it bring you on your Knees before
" God, afterward begin every Action
" of the Day, and attend you to the
" End. Sitting, walking, writing, have
" it always, as it were, waiting at the
" Door of your Heart, and of your
" Mouth; when you kneel to pray, and
" when you rise, and when you go to
" any Thing else, let this be your atten-
" tive and perpetual Prayer." *Cassian*
adds (28), that himself and all the
Monks of the Desert of *Scete*, who af-
sisted at the Discourses of the holy Abbot *Isaac*, admired exceedingly the Prudence of this Instruction, and were sensible from Experience, how much more
easy it is to acquire an Habit of ejacula-
tory Prayer, by having in the Beginning
some devout Form of Aspiration always
at Hand, than in Time of spiritual Dryness to be left at a Loss to call forth one
suitable. Many indeed chuse to make
some other more familiar. St. *Macarius*
recommended this: " Lord, as thou art
" pleased,

(28) Coll. x. c. 14.

"pleased, and seest best, have Mercy
"on me." St. *Thais* the Penitent made
use of this: "Thou who createdest me,
"have Mercy on me." Many have
made Choice of some Petition of the
Lord's Prayer, and numberless others
might be collected from the Practices of
the Saints. That of Abbot *Isaac*, mentioned by *Cassian*, is used by the Church
in the Beginning of every Canonical Hour,
because we can neither open our Hearts
nor our Lips to pray, without the actual
Assistance of divine Grace, and if we invoke the divine Succour in every Action,
much more when we prepare ourselves to
offer to God the Homage of Love and
Praise, and to implore his Mercy and
Blessings. As often as we begin a new
Action, meet with any Success or Disappointment, any Difficulty or Temptation,
as often as we hear the Clock strike, or
at least so frequently as not to interrupt
long the Practice, we ought fervently to
renew in our Hearts our accustomed Aspiration, or some other which our Devotion shall suggest. But in this, and in
every Part of Prayer, the capital Point
is, that we inwardly feel the Sentiments
of the Prayer, be deeply penetrated with
them,

them, and bring them forth from the bottom of our Hearts with unutterable Earnestness, or *Groans*, and *Sighs* in Desire. *Rom.* viii. 26.

Thus will a Soul advance in holy Prayer, and by its Means in all interiour Virtue. For the Holy Ghost will enlarge daily the Kingdom of his Grace and Love in her Affections, subduing, enlightening, purifying and sanctifying them more and more by his Presence. Here he will place His Delight in her Heart, as in His living Temple and Sanctuary, and will not cease to display with unbounded Tenderness and Liberality, the Treasures of His Grace, enriching her more and more with all spiritual feeling Knowledge of his Mysteries and Love, and of her own Nothingness and Miseries. Amongst his various Gifts, those of the most perfect infused Humility and Charity, and Spirit of Prayer, ever hold the first Place. In the Distribution of these Graces, which he diversifies according to his infinite Wisdom, *dividing to every one as he pleases*, he often favours the Soul with the sublime passive Prayer of Union, which Abbot *Isaac*, and from him *Cassian* describes

scribes in the following Words (29). "So "(*i. e.* by thefe Steps) the Mind may be "raifed to that Singlenefs of fpiritual "Prayer, which is not only freed from "all Reprefentation of Images, but alfo "is not diftinguifhed by any Ufe of "Voice, Words, or any of the Senfes, "but is poured forth inwardly by a "flaming Ardour and Intenfenefs of Mind, "(through an unutterable Vehemence of "Affection, and an invincible and in- "conceivable Quicknefs and Alacrity of "Spirit) which the Mind, abftracted "from all Senfes, and material or fenfi- "ble Things, pours forth to God by "Sighs and Groans that cannot be ex- "preffed."

In this Manner Penance and Prayer by their progreffive Exercifes, difpofe our Souls to become the fpiritual Kingdom of God, in which he is pleafed to reign, governing all their Powers and Affections by his fovereign Love, and omnipotent Grace. Thefe holy Exercifes form the myftical Ladder, by which Chriftian Souls afcend to the Summit of all Virtues, and to the City of God, the heavenly *Jerufalem*. Amazing is the Height

---

(29) Ib. c. ii.

on which this Ladder is placed, and to which they aspire. The Dignity, Glory, and Happiness of a Child of God, and an Inhabitant of his Bliss, is altogether incomprehensible to us. How exalted soever this State is, we through the divine Grace are capable of it, and created for it. Yes, mortal and sinful Creatures, as we are, we are called by God to be cleansed from the Filth of Sin, and all irregular Appetites, to conquer our Passions and spiritual Enemies, to be adorned with all Virtues, and to be equalled and associated to the Angels in everlasting Glory. To be admitted into the Kingdom of God, where he reigns with his Saints, the most spotless Purity of Soul and Affections is required, together with the Assemblage of all perfect Virtues. The Height of this glorious and happy State ought not to discourage us, but to animate and spur us on with Fervour. So many Saints have fought and conquered before us; so many hold out their Hands, sweetly inviting us to tread in their Steps, and faithfully follow them in this glorious Path, in which they assure us we shall find the sovereign Good, with sovereign Comfort and Joy.

FINIS.

The Author designs to add an Appendix concerning Religious Orders in general, and therefore the Purchasers of this Work are desired to wait a few Months before they get it bound.

www.ingramcontent.com/pod-product-compliance
Lightning Source LLC
Chambersburg PA
CBHW021727220426
43662CB00008B/732